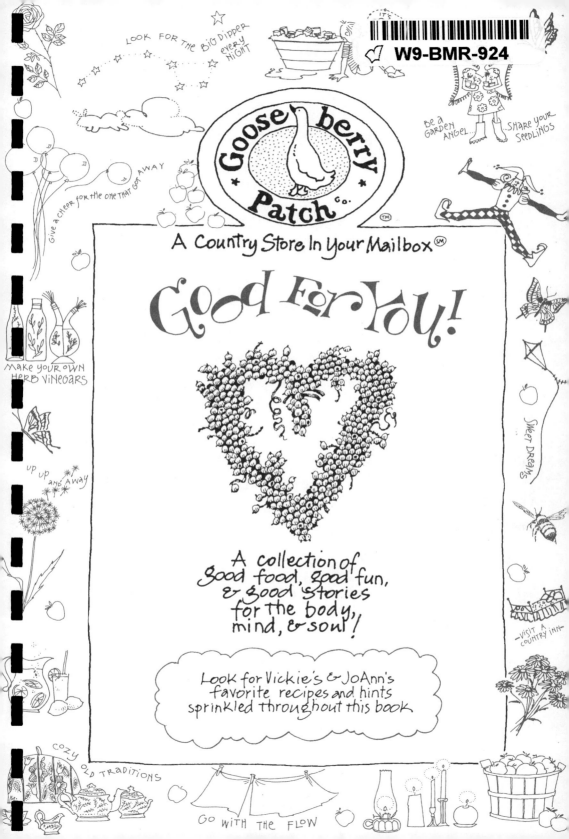

W9-BMR-924

LOOK FOR THE BiG DiPPER every NiGHT

Be a GARDEN ANGeL... SHARE YouR SEEDLiNGS

Give a cHeer for the one THAT Got AwAY

MAKe YOUR OWN HERB ViNeGARS

UP UP AND AWAY

Sweet Dreams

VISIT A COUNTRY INN

COZY OLD TRADITIONS

GO WITH THE FLOW

Goose berry Patch co. ™

A Country Store In Your Mailbox ℠

Good For You!

A collection of good food, good fun, & good stories for the body, mind, & soul!

Look for Vickie's & JoAnn's favorite recipes and hints sprinkled throughout this book

A Country Store In Your Mailbox℠

Gooseberry Patch
149 Johnson Drive
Department BOOK
Delaware, OH 43015
★

1-800-85-GOOSE
1-800-854-6673

Copyright 1996, Gooseberry Patch
0-9632978-8-0
Third Printing, September 1997

How To Subscribe

Would you like to receive
"A Country Store in Your Mailbox"℠?
For a 2-year subscription to our Gooseberry Patch catalog, simply send $3.00 to:

Gooseberry Patch
P.O. Box 190 Dept. BOOK
Delaware, OH 43015

This book is printed on recycled paper.

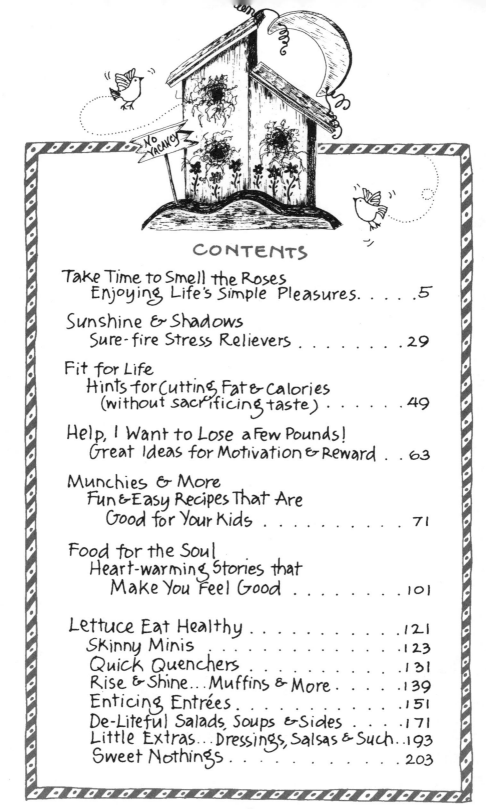

CONTENTS

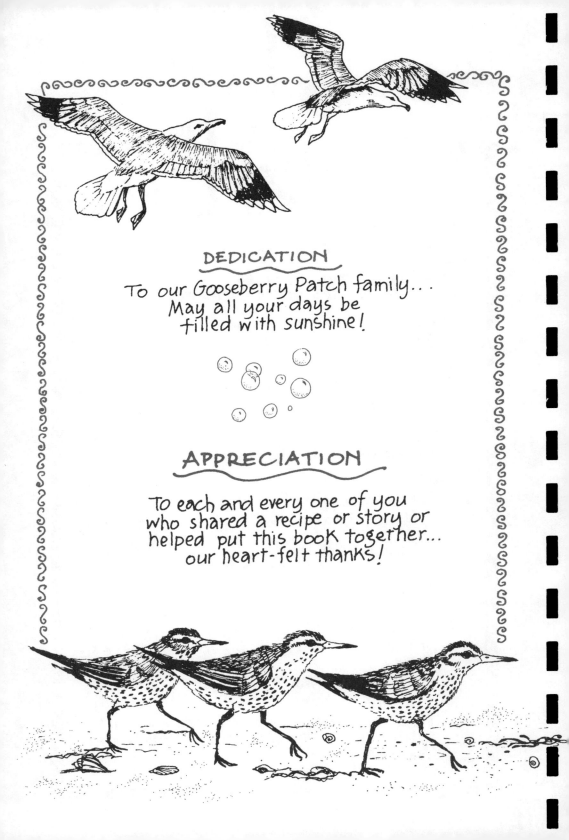

DEDICATION

To our Gooseberry Patch family...
May all your days be
filled with sunshine!

APPRECIATION

To each and every one of you
who shared a recipe or story or
helped put this book together...
our heart-felt thanks!

Take Time to Smell the Roses

Enjoying life's simple pleasures

Take Time to Smell the Roses

To add some health to your romance, try setting a date with your mate for intimate evening strolls. Try this once a week or more if your time allows. Make sure you hold hands when you go for your strolls!

Jeanne Calkins
Midland, MI

Your life is a gift...live it wisely!

Take time to relax and enjoy your life. Don't worry about things that you have no control over. Enjoy your memories as they happen, as well as later when they really are memories. Learn to relax with laughter; it is a great way to eliminate stress. Be able to laugh at yourself.

Look at each event of your life as an ADVENTURE, and you will enjoy it more. If the event is something you don't understand or are afraid of, treating it as an adventure can make it easier to deal with. Also, by treating an event this way, you can change your whole perspective and probably will learn more, as well as enjoy the event more. I always tell children that we are going on an adventure when we go to the Illinois State Fair or to flea markets, craft shows, antique shows, or even a trip to the grocery store, and they always seem to enjoy the idea. The word "adventure" makes it sound exciting.

As you live your life, try to be careful that you won't have regrets later for not doing something. Spend as much time with your loved ones as possible. Too often, we spend more time with co-workers, fellow students and strangers than we do with family. Time is one of our most precious gifts, and we need to use it wisely.

Life can be so exciting! So much to see, so much to learn, so much to be thankful for! Don't fall into a rut; reach for something new to learn.

Mary Ann Nemecek
Springfield, IL

It's nice to do things for others, especially those less fortunate. Take fresh fruit to a nursing home. Since most nursing homes serve frozen, canned and processed foods, fresh fruit is a rare treat. Unlike cookies and other treats, all of the residents, including diabetics, can enjoy fresh fruit. Take apples oranges, pears, seedless grapes and especially bananas. These gifts will be greatly appreciated and will make you feel good inside.

Becky Malone

To treat yourself to "sweet dreams," try making a strong infusion with your favorite dried herbs. Make at least a gallon using lavender, rose geranium, lemon balm, rosemary or any of your favorites, alone or in combinations. Add this herbal water (strained) to the final rinse when you wash your sheets and pillow cases. Then hang your bedding in the sun to dry!

Barbara Bargdill
Gooseberry Patch Personal Shopper

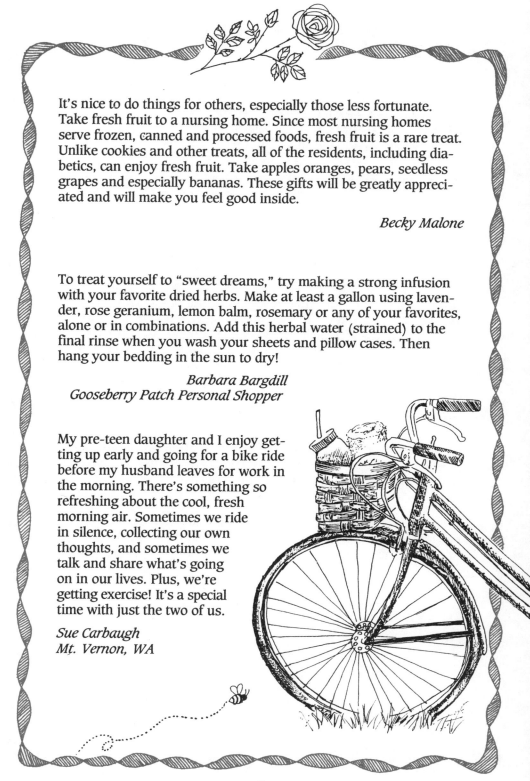

My pre-teen daughter and I enjoy getting up early and going for a bike ride before my husband leaves for work in the morning. There's something so refreshing about the cool, fresh morning air. Sometimes we ride in silence, collecting our own thoughts, and sometimes we talk and share what's going on in our lives. Plus, we're getting exercise! It's a special time with just the two of us.

Sue Carbaugh
Mt. Vernon, WA

Take Time to Smell the Roses

It's fun to stay in touch with the universe. Adopt a constellation. The ones that are easy to spot are Casseopeia, Orion, of course, The Big Dipper and the Little one. And look for them every night. Or every Tuesday.

Never underestimate the power of a popsicle to cool, refresh and make you feel like a kid again. Orange is the hands-down best flavor.

Rearranging furniture always makes me feel good, even if it's only another old ladderback chair I've brought down from the attic and introduced into the living room, or just a couple of scatter rugs I've switched.

Sometimes you just have to throw out all your potholders and start anew. I pick up handmade holders at local church fairs and stash them in the back of a kitchen drawer, awaiting the time when it's finally the moment to chuck out the old and bring on the new. It's as much a gift to the kitchen as to yourself. The same goes for burner "bibs" or the drip pans that fit under electric stove burners. Replacing those all at once is like Christmas.

Take a break from grocery shopping for a week and see how long you can get by, using just the stuff at hand in the pantry, cupboards, freezer, or garden. The rarest meals come out of this kind of non-planning, and you'll enjoy the challenge. It helps to have the rest of your family on your side in this endeavor.

A little rug in the kitchen is wonderful, cozy and luxurious. It can be an old oriental, a new rag rug, a worn braided rug...even a modern-looking kitchen puts on a country face with soft, comfy touches like this. It makes you feel elegant and countrified at the same time.

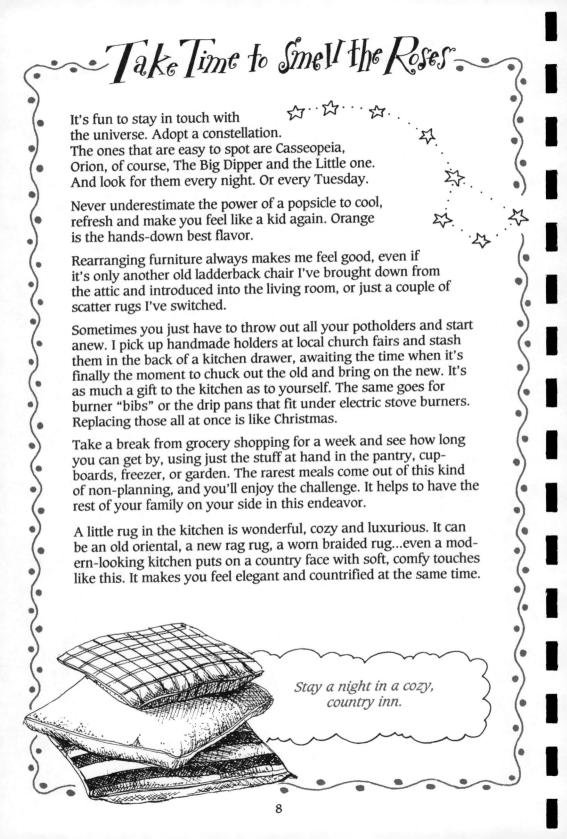

Stay a night in a cozy, country inn.

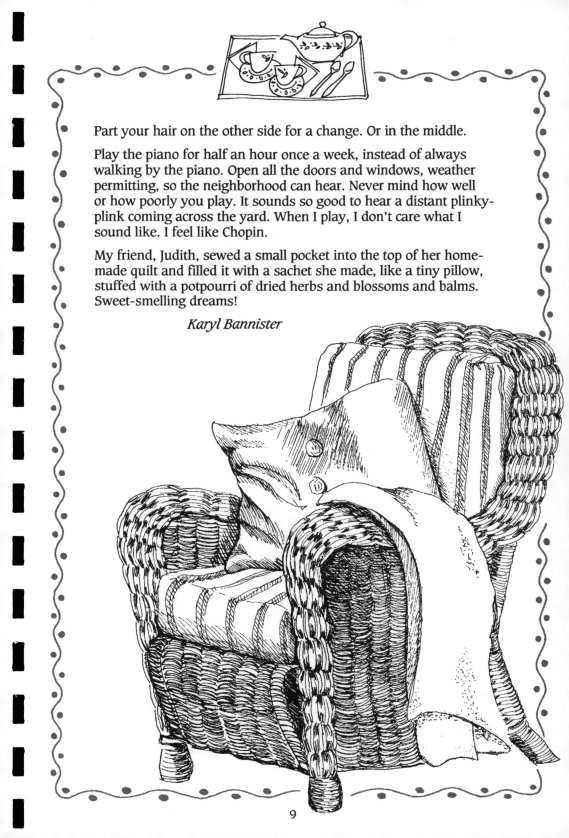

Part your hair on the other side for a change. Or in the middle.

Play the piano for half an hour once a week, instead of always walking by the piano. Open all the doors and windows, weather permitting, so the neighborhood can hear. Never mind how well or how poorly you play. It sounds so good to hear a distant plinky-plink coming across the yard. When I play, I don't care what I sound like. I feel like Chopin.

My friend, Judith, sewed a small pocket into the top of her home-made quilt and filled it with a sachet she made, like a tiny pillow, stuffed with a potpourri of dried herbs and blossoms and balms. Sweet-smelling dreams!

Karyl Bannister

Take Time to Smell the Roses

I run a small business out of my home as well as being a pretty busy mom. Between these two-action packed duties, I sometimes don't get out of the house except to car pool, go to the bus stop or to hit the local copy store! I've always been a fairly social person, and this hibernation can start to get to me after a while. As a result, a few years ago I called upon a few of my sisters and girlfriends and initiated "Girls' Night Out"! Each and every Thursday night, a small group of women get together at a casual restaurant for dinner. We discuss our jobs, families, funny stories, current events, and anything that's important to us. It's really a great thing to look forward to each week. I find myself purposely saving stories for "GNO," and others have been known to copy articles and similar items to share. It's kind of like show & tell for adults! It's also a great way to get out of the house and share the company of other adults...just a few hours of freedom each week!

Joanne Martin-Robinson

When that beautiful song is playing on the car radio, and you have just driven into your driveway, sit a moment and listen until the end before turning off the engine and running into the house.

Get up early and watch the sunrise, while enjoying a hot cup of coffee or tea.

Pat Akers
Stanton, CA

Take time out for a picnic!
Make a quick and easy salad with bow-tie pasta,
flaked salmon, green onions and blanched peas. Toss with
low-cal Italian dressing. Serve crusty french bread, melon,
prosciutto, and a dry white wine (or chilled, sparkling water)
alongside and let the world go by.

Pack up the kids, husband or some friends and get away for the day. It's a great way to get an inexpensive break. Each October, my children and I head out for a 2 1/2 hour trip to a Mennonite auction. We leave early, after stopping off for a latté for the road! I put in our Shaker tapes and we head off on an adventure. We find the most wonderful foods (green bean soup, pies, kraut runze, pfefferneusse and fresh sausage). The children get to watch apple butter being made over an open fire and cornmeal and wheat being ground. There are booths and an incredible auction with gorgeous quilts from all over the United States. We head home with our treasures and another country memory to see us through the winter. The point is this...there are plenty of adventures, festivals, auctions and events within driving distance.

Read the entertainment section of your local paper. Make the effort to be festive! Turn on the music, dress up, bring a basket with a pretty tablecloth and leave the stress behind. Enjoy yourself and your family! It is a choice you will never regret.

Beth
St. Hilaire
Harrah, WA

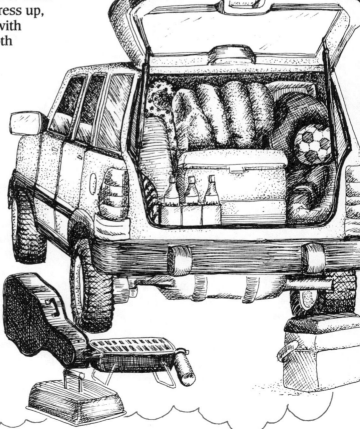

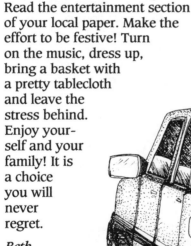

Take Time to Smell the Roses

We vacation for a week in Yosemite National Park each fall. It is so wonderful to have a whole week to unwind! There are free shuttles throughout the valley, so driving our car is totally unnecessary. One fall, my friend and I decided to try not to use the shuttle at all. If we wanted to go somewhere, we would either hike, walk or ride our bikes! It was easier than we thought. The only problem we had was riding our bikes at night without a light! When we had gone to dinner it was still light out, but when we finished, it was really dark. Imagine two grown women riding bikes in the dark with pocket flashlights in their mouths, lighting the way! We still laugh about that vacation. And now we have bike lights!

When my family went on vacation, we either went to the mountain cabin or the beach. No matter where we went, we never had a TV or radio. Instead, we had an old 8-track tape player on which we listened to show tunes and big band music. For entertainment we played cards, memory games or read books and magazines. We made up skits; we sang songs. We walked to town to buy pastries for breakfast and fresh bread for lunch and dinner. We window shopped. We ate and played. The time went quickly, yet these trips are what memories are made of. We had a blast!

When my aunt, uncle and cousins came to town, it was always a grand time at our house. My aunt would bring her ukulele. We would sit on the kitchen floor and sing "Ain't She Sweet?," "Little Grass Shack," "When the Saints Come Marching In" and "Michael Row the Boat Ashore," to name a few. It may have sounded like the Mitch Miller Drop-Outs, but we sure had fun!

More and more, our daily lives have become so structured, so scheduled, that we have left no time for the fun, spontaneous activities that we love to do! Once in a while, I will receive a call from my husband at the office. He tells me that he has called "Camp Grandma" to make a reservation for our son to spend the night, and that we are going out to see a movie and have dinner! My practical side reminds me that I have laundry to do, dust bunnies to corral, and maybe, dishes left to do. But just as quickly, my "footloose" side says, "The laundry, dust bunnies and dishes will wait!" Boy, did this take some conditioning on my part!

After dinner during the summer, sometimes my mom and my sisters and I would gather on the kitchen floor (it was cooler there) to play jacks. It was fun to play together, even when the younger ones struggled to coordinate the jacks and ball pickup. Lots of laughter could be heard coming from the kitchen. Believe it or not, after all these years, I still have the old metal jacks and petrified rubber balls!

Some of my favorite sayings...

"Don't sweat the small stuff!" Flo Bond

"It's not the pace of life that concerns me. It's the sudden stop at the end!" Unknown

"May all your weeds be wildflowers." Unknown

"Life is about learning to relax your expectations." Peg Ackerman

"Tomorrow is a brand new day...with no mistakes!" Anne Shirley

Peg Ackerman
Pasadena, CA

The simplest pleasures are the best, like...

Sitting by a fire on a winter afternoon
Slipping under flannel sheets on a cold winter's night
Curling up with the Sunday paper
Listening to children at play
Picking the summer's first tomato
Watching fireflies blinking across the yard
The smell of just-cut grass
Watching a small-town parade
An old-fashioned hayride
Having a good laugh!
The first snow of winter
Coming home.

Mary K. Murray
Mount Vernon, OH

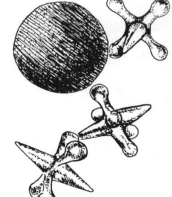

Take Time to Smell the Roses

When my husband and I were first dating, we would go to the local flea market bright and early on a Sunday morning. We would browse around and purchase goodies for my "hopeless chest." We would also buy some cheese and pepperoni sticks. Then we would jump back into the car and head out to the country. We would travel all the back roads, nibble on our cheese and stop at all the farm stands along the way. When we arrived back home, we would have a car full of fresh produce, wildflowers, and memories of a wonderful afternoon.

Marie Alana Gardner
North Tonawanda, NY

Practice Earth Day everyday. Be conscious of the products you purchase and their effect on the environment. Visit your local health food store and become acquainted with the array of products they carry which are not harmful to the environment. Recycle any packaging that is recyclable. Ask your grocery store to stock products that have not been tested on animals. Take a canvas bag or two to the grocery store, and everywhere you go, so you won't need the store bags for your purchases. Practice "saving a tree" every chance you get. Remember, a healthy life includes a healthy planet.

Nancie Gensler
Walnut Creek, CA

Create a gift basket with low-fat and low-cholesterol foods for a friend who is on a diet. This is a good gift for a birthday or as a hostess gift.

Walk or ride bikes with a friend.

Take a friend to lunch on her birthday.

Plan a covered dish dinner and have everyone bring a low-fat dish.

Marion Pfeifer
Smyrna, DE

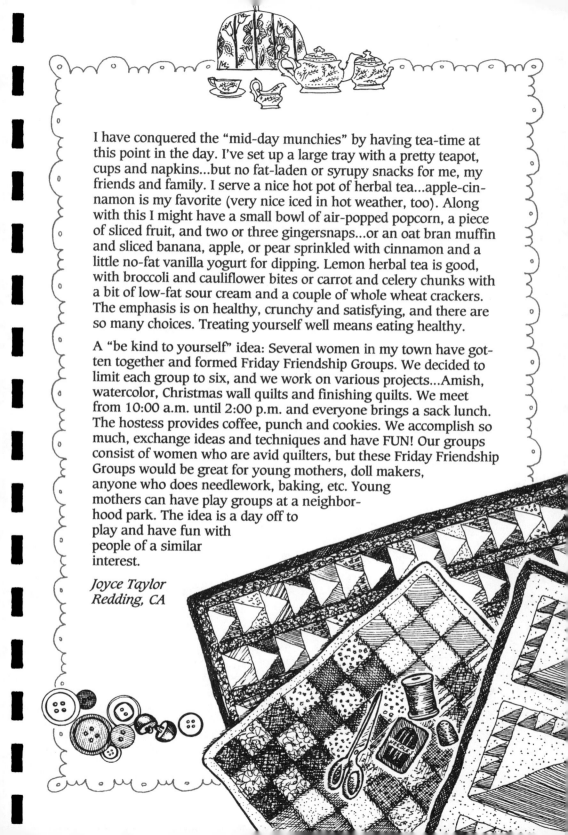

I have conquered the "mid-day munchies" by having tea-time at this point in the day. I've set up a large tray with a pretty teapot, cups and napkins...but no fat-laden or syrupy snacks for me, my friends and family. I serve a nice hot pot of herbal tea...apple-cinnamon is my favorite (very nice iced in hot weather, too). Along with this I might have a small bowl of air-popped popcorn, a piece of sliced fruit, and two or three gingersnaps...or an oat bran muffin and sliced banana, apple, or pear sprinkled with cinnamon and a little no-fat vanilla yogurt for dipping. Lemon herbal tea is good, with broccoli and cauliflower bites or carrot and celery chunks with a bit of low-fat sour cream and a couple of whole wheat crackers. The emphasis is on healthy, crunchy and satisfying, and there are so many choices. Treating yourself well means eating healthy.

A "be kind to yourself" idea: Several women in my town have gotten together and formed Friday Friendship Groups. We decided to limit each group to six, and we work on various projects...Amish, watercolor, Christmas wall quilts and finishing quilts. We meet from 10:00 a.m. until 2:00 p.m. and everyone brings a sack lunch. The hostess provides coffee, punch and cookies. We accomplish so much, exchange ideas and techniques and have FUN! Our groups consist of women who are avid quilters, but these Friday Friendship Groups would be great for young mothers, doll makers, anyone who does needlework, baking, etc. Young mothers can have play groups at a neighborhood park. The idea is a day off to play and have fun with people of a similar interest.

Joyce Taylor
Redding, CA

Take Time to Smell the Roses

Put on your favorite music and dance! Not only good for your spirit, but good for your heart!

Go for a drive in the country and play your favorite tape in the car. Sing along as loud as you want!

Relax...go outside on a clear night and look at the moon and the stars with a telescope or binoculars. Gather the whole family and have a hot dog/marshmallow roast at the same time.

Once a year, get together with your friends and go on a retreat without husbands and kids! Do something as grand as going on a cruise or simply rent a condo at a nearby lake...stay in your gowns all day, go antique shopping, etc. The point is to do what you want to do.

Quarreling with someone? Remember, life is too short. Most arguments aren't worthy of all the time and energy people put into them.

Be forgiving of yourself and others.

Do something nice for someone and never tell them it was you. You will both get a warm feeling in your heart.

Don't waste time and energy worrying about past mistakes. Pick yourself up by your boot straps and move on.

Constantly show your family and friends how much they mean to you. These are the people that make your life worth living.

Feel something is missing in your life? Become a volunteer. There are plenty of organizations that need your help...Humane Society, Children's Hospitals, Big Brothers/Big Sisters, homeless shelters, and many other worthy organizations.

Joy Daniel
Roland, AR

Put Christmas music on the stereo during the "dog days" of summer. Sit down for a few minutes with a cool drink and think "snow."

Yvonne Van Brimmer
Lompoc, CA

Music is such a natural "pick-me-up." Play your favorite tunes when ironing, washing the car, sewing, gardening, cooking or any activity where you can hum or tap your toes. Funny, I seem to iron faster when I listen to music!

In order to keep up with the current book best sellers or classic favorites, I get audio books from the library and listen to them while baking or doing the dishes. I feel I am accomplishing two significant tasks at once. This also works great if you want to learn a new language or brush up on your high school Spanish!

Debbie Benjamin

Close your eyes and listen to the sounds of nature...
crickets chirping, doves cooing, geese honking, bees buzzing.
It's quite a performance, and it's all for free!

Take Time to Smell the Roses

Line dry your linens...a better night's sleep cannot be had! The warm sun and airy breezes make the sheets and blankets feel almost starched and ironed. Saves on the utility bills also!

Tuck a small bundle of lavender among linens that are to be stored. The scent is fresh and clean and an extra delight in the winter to remind you of the garden.

Take time to relax and stay in bed a bit longer. Curl up in bed and read, and listen to the birds outside your window. Sometimes the birds pattering across my roof sound like gentle rain. After sleeping late, relax in a hot scented bath. Use fragrant herbal "teas" for the bath. Your favorite herbs are tied into a muslin or cheesecloth square and secured with a rubber band or ribbon. Tie the herbal bundle under the faucet so the hot water can infuse the fragrant oils into your bath water. Another fragrant bath is to make "salts" with Epsom salts and a fragrant oil essence. Use 2 cups Epsom salts and 3 drops of your favorite oil. (I prefer lavender.) Allow to sit uninterrupted in a covered jar for one week before using. To use in bath, pour 1/4 cup into hot bath water (or more if you desire).

Everyone needs a tree swing, the simplest and most wonderful of garden pleasures. Ours is hanging from an old pecan tree that over-looks my perennial garden. Kids love to swing and try to reach the very spot where the green earth ends and blue sky begins. For me, a swing is an absolute necessity. I hope I never outgrow swinging!

Plant your own "rag gourd." Imagine washing with a squash! Loofahs make wonderful vines to watch growing, and when the cucumber-like fruits are ripe, you have a scrub for rough elbows and heels. They make excellent gifts to tuck into a basket with floral or herbal soaps for hot baths.

Read a book of poems or, better yet, start collecting poems for your own enjoyment. I enjoy jotting down favorite quotes and poems into a personal journal. You could even carry a small note-book in your purse, too. One of my favorite quotes is, "Some people are always grumbling that roses have thorns; I am thankful that thorns have roses." Alphonse Karr (1808-1890), French writer and editor. Be on the lookout... quotes, cute phrases, and poems appear in overlooked places.

Make a windchime to enjoy in the garden. Use old silverware, flattened somewhat by a rubber mallet. Drill a small hole for a hanging cord. Fishing line works great for hangers. Hang silverware at various heights and lengths. The top hanger for the fishing line can be a fork on which each tine has been alternately bent.

My favorite relaxation technique is to sit in my antique wicker rocker and cross-stitch. Needlework provides excellent relaxation. Stitching with scented candle burning and a cup of hot herbal tea or apple cider completes the setting.

Take the last edible blossoms before your first freeze and preserve them to enjoy later. Freeze them in ice trays with water. We enjoy iced drinks even in winter here in Texas! The frozen blossoms look great in herbal tea and lemonade.

Press small flowers and use later to make book markers to give as gifts. Great to have on hand to give a friend along with a book or magazine.

If you are like me and enjoy the seaside, but do not live close by, decorate your own seaside room. I'm currently decorating a room with a "seaside theme." The walls are decorated with a lighthouse stencil. I'm using lots of sailboat-themed pillows, prints, etc. To pull the room together, I'm using seashells in baskets and bowls and even covering an ugly old table lamp with rope to give it a nautical theme. I plan to use the room for instant pick-me-ups this winter on dark, cold days.

Surprise your family and do things out of season! When it is too cold for a picnic outdoors, have one inside! Have lemonade and watermelon in January! Why limit picnics to the daylight hours? Plan a picnic after sundown. Choose a spot where star watching will be at its best. Star constellations can be reproduced at home with glow-in-the-dark stickers placed strategically on ceilings. I've done this for my children and, no matter how old they get, they still enjoy turning out their lights at night.

Jeannine English
Wylie, TX

I love to bake and give things away as gifts to our friends. I try to make up a tin or basket of their favorite things. This gives me such a good feeling, and makes them happy too! It's a true gift of love from the oven.

Even though my husband and I don't have children old enough for our church youth group, we have headed it for the past two years. We enjoy working with these young people. I guess it's because we've never grown up ourselves!

Kimberly Burns

I enjoy getting up early Saturday mornings, fixing a cup of tea and going out to sit on the deck. Everything is so peaceful and relaxing. We enjoy the birds and feed them year 'round. We live in the country and have several pine trees in our yard that the red birds love to perch in and sing to their mates. Our clematis vines and gladiolus attract the hummingbirds and they are such a delight!

We enjoy having our grandchildren over for the weekends. We fly kites, take walks, and go on picnics. Children keep us young. They're always full of energy, smiles and hugs (things we all need).

Sharon Hall
Gooseberry Patch Warehouse

Candlelight, china and crystal make any low-cal meal more exciting. And don't forget the flowers. They make your room beautiful, and you'll feel very special.

Deb Weiser
Gooseberry Patch Warehouse

Start a daily ritual of exercise at home...
same time every day.
Set yourself up with a floor-length mirror,
proper clothes, music, favorite TV show...
whatever works for you.

I like to make a good cup of red clover tea with a teaspoon of honey and browse through my idea book. I save all the catalogs that come all year 'round. After Christmas I make a fire, sip my tea and, with my trusty old scissors, I begin to cut out pictures of decorating ideas I like. I put these pictures on black construction paper with a glue stick...trying to keep Christmas pictures all on one sheet and Easter ideas on another sheet, etc. Then I take them and laminate each construction sheet. I take a 3-ring hole punch and punch holes in the construction paper that's been laminated. I then put them in a large notebook. I have done this now for 3 years. Everyone loves to look at this special book of mine. I always get a lift when I look at the creative ideas that inspired me when I first looked at the catalogs. Cutting with scissors on paper has always made me happy. I loved it as a child...and I still do.

In our women's Bible study, one of our assignments on a series "You are Beautiful" was to take a candlelit bath and totally relax! I had never taken a candlelit bath or even a bath just for fun. Baths were taken only when I was ill, to pull out toxins from the body and to breathe in the moist air. This was so unusual for me, but I knew I had to do the assignment before all of us ladies met back again next week. So I put a vanilla-scented candle on the bathtub ledge and went a step further and added a large orange, peelings and all. I took the large peels in my hands and rubbed them on my arms and legs. I was surprised at how soothing it felt. And oh, the smell of vanilla mixed with fresh oranges! It took me back to my childhood...when we used to stop the ice cream truck (my favorite ice cream bar was called a 50-50 bar, vanilla ice cream covered with an orange-flavored juice). The fragrance of this bath was just like the taste of a 50-50 bar. I'm glad I did the assignment...and I have continued to partake in this delightful way of pampering myself even when I'm not ill.

Linda Tatman
Fresno, CA

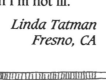

Take Time to Smell the Roses

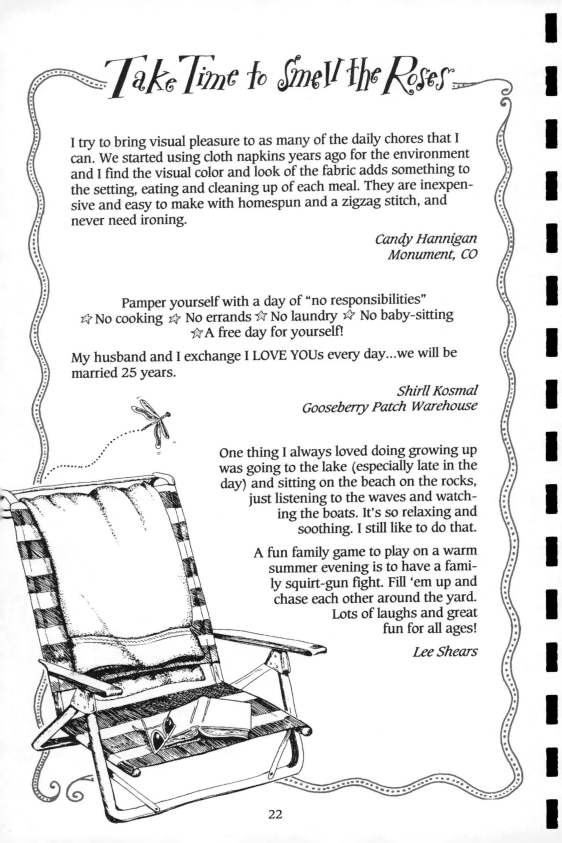

I try to bring visual pleasure to as many of the daily chores that I can. We started using cloth napkins years ago for the environment and I find the visual color and look of the fabric adds something to the setting, eating and cleaning up of each meal. They are inexpensive and easy to make with homespun and a zigzag stitch, and never need ironing.

Candy Hannigan
Monument, CO

Pamper yourself with a day of "no responsibilities"
☆ No cooking ☆ No errands ☆ No laundry ☆ No baby-sitting
☆ A free day for yourself!

My husband and I exchange I LOVE YOUs every day...we will be married 25 years.

Shirll Kosmal
Gooseberry Patch Warehouse

One thing I always loved doing growing up was going to the lake (especially late in the day) and sitting on the beach on the rocks, just listening to the waves and watching the boats. It's so relaxing and soothing. I still like to do that.

A fun family game to play on a warm summer evening is to have a family squirt-gun fight. Fill 'em up and chase each other around the yard. Lots of laughs and great fun for all ages!

Lee Shears

22

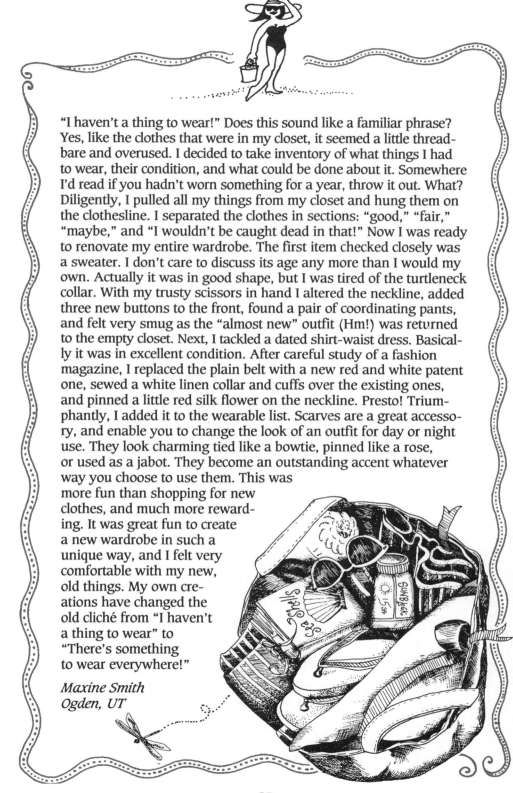

"I haven't a thing to wear!" Does this sound like a familiar phrase? Yes, like the clothes that were in my closet, it seemed a little threadbare and overused. I decided to take inventory of what things I had to wear, their condition, and what could be done about it. Somewhere I'd read if you hadn't worn something for a year, throw it out. What? Diligently, I pulled all my things from my closet and hung them on the clothesline. I separated the clothes in sections: "good," "fair," "maybe," and "I wouldn't be caught dead in that!" Now I was ready to renovate my entire wardrobe. The first item checked closely was a sweater. I don't care to discuss its age any more than I would my own. Actually it was in good shape, but I was tired of the turtleneck collar. With my trusty scissors in hand I altered the neckline, added three new buttons to the front, found a pair of coordinating pants, and felt very smug as the "almost new" outfit (Hm!) was returned to the empty closet. Next, I tackled a dated shirt-waist dress. Basically it was in excellent condition. After careful study of a fashion magazine, I replaced the plain belt with a new red and white patent one, sewed a white linen collar and cuffs over the existing ones, and pinned a little red silk flower on the neckline. Presto! Triumphantly, I added it to the wearable list. Scarves are a great accessory, and enable you to change the look of an outfit for day or night use. They look charming tied like a bowtie, pinned like a rose, or used as a jabot. They become an outstanding accent whatever way you choose to use them. This was more fun than shopping for new clothes, and much more rewarding. It was great fun to create a new wardrobe in such a unique way, and I felt very comfortable with my new, old things. My own creations have changed the old cliché from "I haven't a thing to wear" to "There's something to wear everywhere!"

Maxine Smith
Ogden, UT

Take Time to Smell the Roses

These are a few of my thoughts from my own personal journal:

Doing your best is far more important than being the best.

What gives your life value isn't what you can do but what you are.

Live well, laugh often and love much.

Let your life be an inspiration to others.

Set high goals, be the best you can be and don't let anyone tell you what you can't be.

The warming sunshine of family and friends make our days very special.

Raise your umbrella and smile after a down day.

We women are born knowing we need one another...loving, caring.

Value that special friend who is near and dear to you.

Sometimes there are no words, only love.

May your day be filled with beauty, your heart with love, your home with joy.

Never forget how much your friends and family love and admire you.

Don't be filled with regret at all the things you failed to say.

May the world always be as beautiful as you make it for others.

The enthusiasm you radiate becomes contagious.

It's how much we enjoy that makes happiness.

When your heart is full of love you always have something to give.

When you understand, accept and love yourself, you are free to be yourself.

SMiLe!

Happy people attract happy people.

Each day is a fresh beginning.

Live today.

Be true to yourself.

Take minute vacations.

The best day is...today.

Forgiveness is the best gift.

Take time to look at one another.

SMiLe WRiNKLes aRe THe BeST KiND

The greatest comfort...work well done.

Be a person who makes things happen.

The most important things happen when you don't look for them.

Let your Light Shine

Value your present moments.
Get in touch with your now.
Be spontaneous and alive.
Be a rock of self-esteem.
"You," make your day.
Learn to live now.
Be a doer.
Let yourself go.
Reach out and grow.
Take mind trips alone.

Be able to do anything at the spur of the second.
Take risks to get you out of your routine.
The sunshine of the soul is laughter.
We all need an umbrella of security.
Don't run away from what you feel.
We won't find time, we have to make it.
We must all find a slower rhythm of life.
Each moment that we live is like a rare perfume.
You create your own special occasion, any day, any time.
You no longer save the best things of life for some distant moment.
Of all the things you wear, your expression is the most important.
We must take time to read, exercise, be alone with friends, and
choose our "wants" over "shoulds" sometimes.
Joy has to be one of the most important goals we have.
Today is your life, not yesterday or tomorrow.

Mary Studer
Gooseberry Patch Warehouse

A "SUNDIAL JOURNAL" RECORDS THE SUNNY HOURS

Take time to daydream.

Take Time to Smell the Roses

I enjoy the very early morning when I can take my devotional book out on the porch. I love the smell and the sounds as the birds, butterflies, and insects are just coming to the herbs and flowers that surround the porch. Starting the day this way makes it go better for me.

At the end of the day, I again go to the porch as the yard turns that beautiful shade of green just before sunset. I once tried to write a poem about this time of day, but it is a feeling that is too beautiful for words. Sometimes a hummingbird will come right up to where I am sitting next to the bee balm. In a busy world, it is so important to just find a quiet place to be alone. Being surrounded with herbs and flowers to touch and smell has made me wonder how, down through the years, man has used plants. When you start to read and learn what an important part these plants have played, you become inspired to learn more about them and use them more. It makes me feel good to be an herbalist and gardener, working with herbs and flowers every day. And, what makes you feel good, must be healthy for you!

An herbal bath is not for getting clean, it is for relaxing and feeling good. After your usual bath or shower, you are ready to pamper yourself with an herbal bath. One way to add herbs and flowers to your bath is using a bath bag. Bath bags can easily be made out of muslin, double cheesecloth or super-fine net. Place the herbs and flowers in the middle of the material, gather up the material and tie, leaving a long string to tie on the faucet. Swish the bag around in the water and rub it over your body.

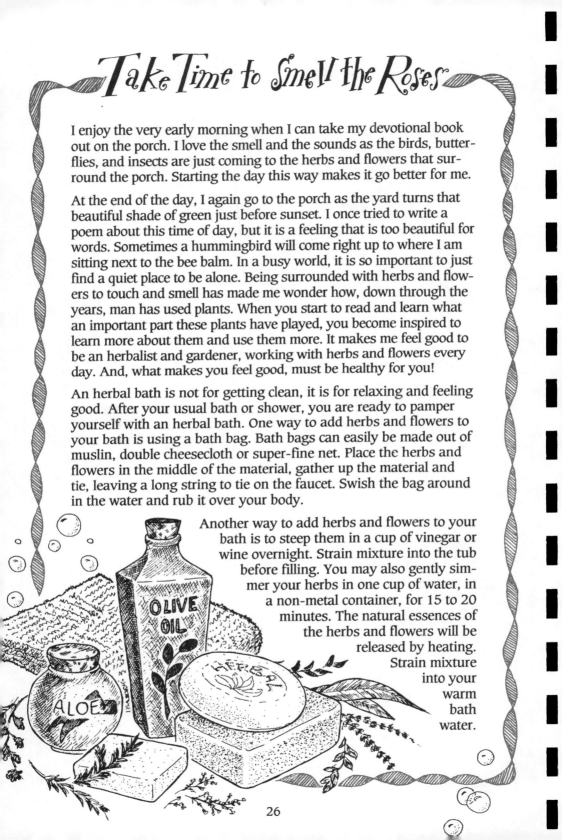

Another way to add herbs and flowers to your bath is to steep them in a cup of vinegar or wine overnight. Strain mixture into the tub before filling. You may also gently simmer your herbs in one cup of water, in a non-metal container, for 15 to 20 minutes. The natural essences of the herbs and flowers will be released by heating. Strain mixture into your warm bath water.

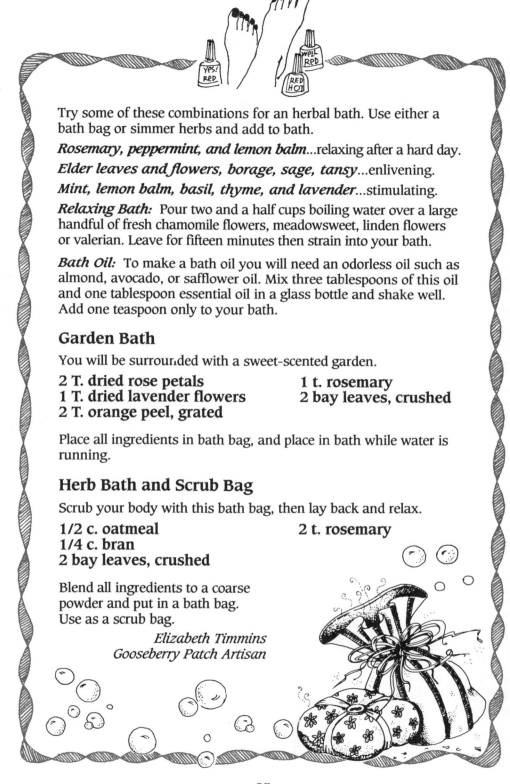

Try some of these combinations for an herbal bath. Use either a bath bag or simmer herbs and add to bath.

Rosemary, peppermint, and lemon balm...relaxing after a hard day.

Elder leaves and flowers, borage, sage, tansy...enlivening.

Mint, lemon balm, basil, thyme, and lavender...stimulating.

Relaxing Bath: Pour two and a half cups boiling water over a large handful of fresh chamomile flowers, meadowsweet, linden flowers or valerian. Leave for fifteen minutes then strain into your bath.

Bath Oil: To make a bath oil you will need an odorless oil such as almond, avocado, or safflower oil. Mix three tablespoons of this oil and one tablespoon essential oil in a glass bottle and shake well. Add one teaspoon only to your bath.

Garden Bath

You will be surrounded with a sweet-scented garden.

2 T. dried rose petals	1 t. rosemary
1 T. dried lavender flowers	2 bay leaves, crushed
2 T. orange peel, grated	

Place all ingredients in bath bag, and place in bath while water is running.

Herb Bath and Scrub Bag

Scrub your body with this bath bag, then lay back and relax.

1/2 c. oatmeal	2 t. rosemary
1/4 c. bran	
2 bay leaves, crushed	

Blend all ingredients to a coarse powder and put in a bath bag. Use as a scrub bag.

Elizabeth Timmins
Gooseberry Patch Artisan

Take Time to Smell the Roses

One of my favorite sayings is, "If it is to be, it's up to me." That applies to my living healthy after a major change in my life.

For a positive life change, learn something new. I went back to college after an absence of 32 years, during which time I raised four wonderful children.

I fell in love with the man in my life when he silently took my hand, led me outdoors and walked joyfully with me in the autumn leaves. Wonderful!

Learn C.P.R. You'll never know when you may need it. Keep a positive attitude about life.

Give yourself "permission" to do the things you enjoy. Spend an hour cross-stitching, reading a book, going for a walk, or doing absolutely nothing!

"Make new friends, keep the old, one is silver, the other is gold."

You can do anything, if you want it badly enough!
☆ Learn a new craft. ☆ Take a cooking class. ☆ Take dancing lessons.
☆ Explore your options.

Nancy Campbell
Bellingham, WA

Make your own herbal bath garden. Plant favorites such as: lemon verbena, rosemary, sage, tansy, peppermint, pennyroyal, lavender, thyme and lemon balm. Use either fresh or dried herbs in a small cloth drawstring bag and tie onto hot water faucet. Scents will invade the room and bath!

Sunshine & Shadows

Sure~fire stress relievers

Herbal Steam

Theresa Nobuyuki
Laguna Hills, CA

Pamper yourself with an herbal steam. Here's all you need...

Hot (not boiling) water
2 c. fresh herbs or 1 c. dried herbs

Place herbs in a bowl, pour in the hot water, and stir well. Drape a towel over your head to trap the steam and steam your face for five minutes.

Herbal suggestions:

Marigold: astringent, cleansing, toning, healing

Lavender: antiseptic, stimulating, toning

Chamomile: cleansing, cooling, soothing

Mint: astringent, cleansing, soothing

Thyme: cleansing, antiseptic, toning

Rosemary: cleansing, stimulating

Fennel: astringent

Herbal Facial Pack
2 T. plain yogurt
1 to 2 T. fine oatmeal
2 T. finely chopped herb leaves
selected according to skin type

Stir the yogurt and herbs together until they are well-blended. Stir in enough oatmeal to form a soft paste and mix well. If you have acne/oily skin, you may want to include 1 to 2 teaspoons of lemon juice to the mixture. For storage, spoon paste into a jar, cover, label, and store in the refrigerator.

Herbal Pillows

Judy Hand
Centre Hall, PA

An herbal pillow brings me peace and tranquility...I make it from trimmings and clippings from my herb garden. As I manicure my gardens, I save all fragrant clippings and flowers. Once dried, I mix them, sometimes adding fragrance oils to complement the aromatic scent, and stuff them into a casing made with fabrics left over from other sewing projects. Fabrics may be fancy or plain; trimmed with

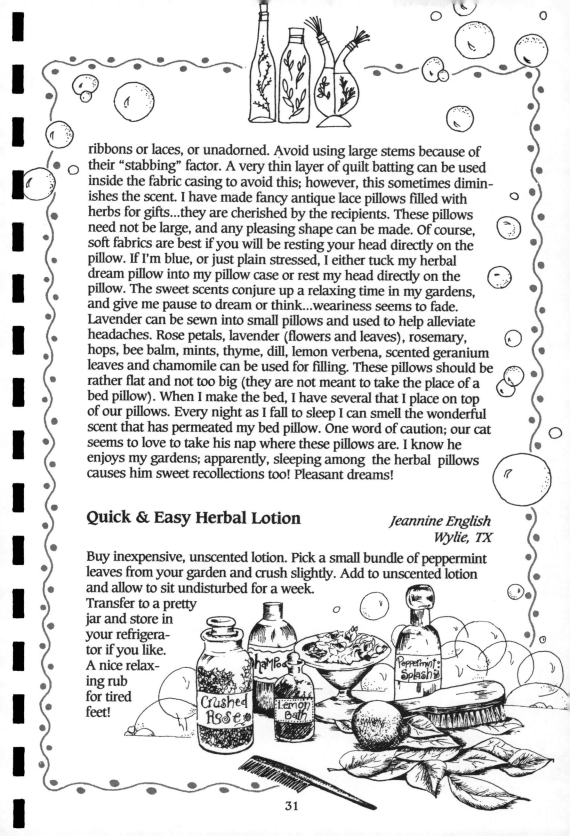

ribbons or laces, or unadorned. Avoid using large stems because of their "stabbing" factor. A very thin layer of quilt batting can be used inside the fabric casing to avoid this; however, this sometimes diminishes the scent. I have made fancy antique lace pillows filled with herbs...they are cherished by the recipients. These pillows need not be large, and any pleasing shape can be made. Of course, soft fabrics are best if you will be resting your head directly on the pillow. If I'm blue, or just plain stressed, I either tuck my herbal dream pillow into my pillow case or rest my head directly on the pillow. The sweet scents conjure up a relaxing time in my gardens, and give me pause to dream or think...weariness seems to fade. Lavender can be sewn into small pillows and used to help alleviate headaches. Rose petals, lavender (flowers and leaves), rosemary, hops, bee balm, mints, thyme, dill, lemon verbena, scented geranium leaves and chamomile can be used for filling. These pillows should be rather flat and not too big (they are not meant to take the place of a bed pillow). When I make the bed, I have several that I place on top of our pillows. Every night as I fall to sleep I can smell the wonderful scent that has permeated my bed pillow. One word of caution; our cat seems to love to take his nap where these pillows are. I know he enjoys my gardens; apparently, sleeping among the herbal pillows causes him sweet recollections too! Pleasant dreams!

Quick & Easy Herbal Lotion

Jeannine English
Wylie, TX

Buy inexpensive, unscented lotion. Pick a small bundle of peppermint leaves from your garden and crush slightly. Add to unscented lotion and allow to sit undisturbed for a week. Transfer to a pretty jar and store in your refrigerator if you like. A nice relaxing rub for tired feet!

Sunshine & Shadows

Here's my favorite prescription for stress relief. Go and buy your favorite bubble bath and scented soap. Do some advance preparation by putting fresh sheets on the bed and laying out your favorite book. Bring the radio (or tape player) and every candle in the house in the bathroom. Then lock yourself in the bathroom away from the world and all its cares. Fill the tub with warm water and lots of bubble bath. While the tub fills, turn on beautiful, soothing music and light lots of candles. Immerse yourself in the bubbles and close your eyes. Then, "whatever is true, whatever is noble, whatever is right, whatever is pure, whatever is lovely, whatever is admirable...if anything is excellent or praiseworthy...think about such things." Phillippians 4:8. Feel the stress leave your body as you renew your mind! Don't feel guilty about lingering! Dry off with your biggest, fluffiest towel. Slather on lots of moisturizer, cream, lotion or after-bath splash, whatever is your favorite, and plop into bed. Put lots of pillows behind your head and feel like a princess. Read until you drift off into dreamland. I promise you will wake the next morning feeling pampered and refreshed. Block time on your calendar for this stress-reliever on a regular basis.

Nancy Marley
Rowlett, TX

After a long, hard day, my husband and I will treat each other to a nice long foot rub and massage with peppermint foot lotion. We really enjoy it, because it's something we can do for one another that makes us feel great.

A great stress-reliever is turning down the lights, putting Yanni on the CD player and just letting your mind go. (Yanni's music is wonderful!)

Lee Shears

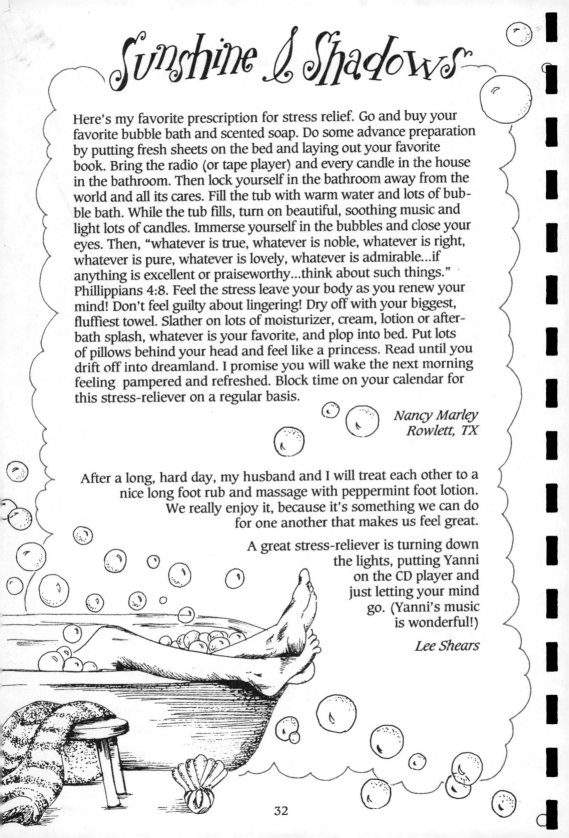

32

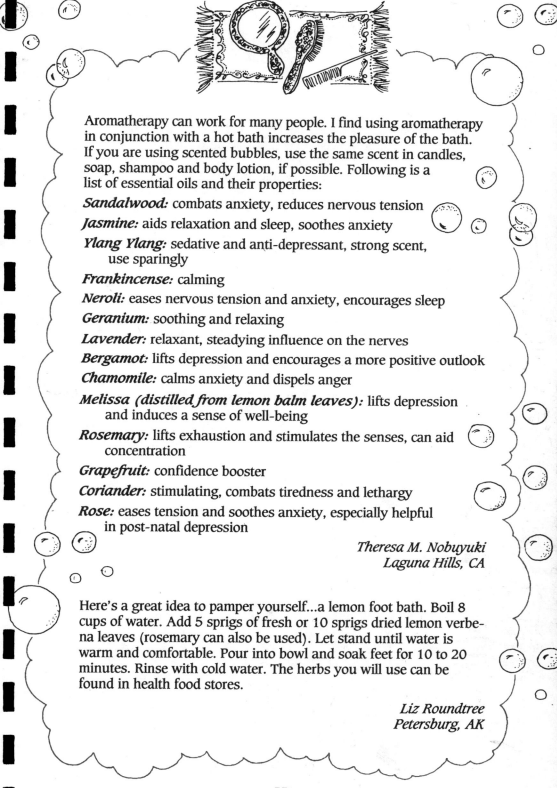

Aromatherapy can work for many people. I find using aromatherapy in conjunction with a hot bath increases the pleasure of the bath. If you are using scented bubbles, use the same scent in candles, soap, shampoo and body lotion, if possible. Following is a list of essential oils and their properties:

Sandalwood: combats anxiety, reduces nervous tension

Jasmine: aids relaxation and sleep, soothes anxiety

Ylang Ylang: sedative and anti-depressant, strong scent, use sparingly

Frankincense: calming

Neroli: eases nervous tension and anxiety, encourages sleep

Geranium: soothing and relaxing

Lavender: relaxant, steadying influence on the nerves

Bergamot: lifts depression and encourages a more positive outlook

Chamomile: calms anxiety and dispels anger

Melissa (distilled from lemon balm leaves): lifts depression and induces a sense of well-being

Rosemary: lifts exhaustion and stimulates the senses, can aid concentration

Grapefruit: confidence booster

Coriander: stimulating, combats tiredness and lethargy

Rose: eases tension and soothes anxiety, especially helpful in post-natal depression

Theresa M. Nobuyuki
Laguna Hills, CA

Here's a great idea to pamper yourself...a lemon foot bath. Boil 8 cups of water. Add 5 sprigs of fresh or 10 sprigs dried lemon verbena leaves (rosemary can also be used). Let stand until water is warm and comfortable. Pour into bowl and soak feet for 10 to 20 minutes. Rinse with cold water. The herbs you will use can be found in health food stores.

Liz Roundtree
Petersburg, AK

Sunshine & Shadows

One of my favorite things to do that helps me relax is to visit the bath and body store. With all of the wonderful smells from the bubble baths and lotions, I immediately begin to relax. I wander around, smelling all the products. Even If I don't really need anything, I always buy something. Then when I get home, I try out my item and then relax in a giant bubble bath. I light some candles and play lazy music and just relax with the warm water and wonderful smells. Soaking away my tensions really helps me to get ready for the next day.

Suzanne Edie

My home is my haven away from the busy outside world, and finding ways to make my house warm and inviting are very important to me. One very special touch I have always used is "scents." Whether it's potpourri or scented candles, I love to fill my home with warm smells. Specific scents evoke special memories. Cinnamon and citrus always remind me of the holidays. Vanilla and spice make me think of baking and happy times with my family. Apple potpourri always finds its way to my wooden bowls in the spring; a promise of good things to come. Natural beeswax candles are my all-time favorite. Their fresh scent really fills the house with a wonderful aroma. Lighting candles makes my Cape Cod farmhouse warm and inviting. It also sets a more relaxed mood in a too busy world. Just sitting quietly watching the fire by candlelight really melts the stress away! I like to put a chunky candle in an old wooden bowl and surround it with potpourri. That way you get "double" the wonderful aromas!

Carol Bull
Gooseberry Patch Personal Shopper

Massage...
so calming and helps
relieve stress.

34

A "SUNDIAL JOURNAL" RECORDS THE SUNNY HOURS

The best stress-buster is to haunt flea markets, antique shops and malls, thrift shops, yard and estate sales. Even if you don't have anything in mind to look for, the looking is a great way to forget your worries. Amid outdated furniture and clothing, you might just find a treasure you can't live without! Every time you see this treasure in your home, you'll remember how much fun you had that day.

Jeannine English
Wylie, TX

I find letter writing to be not only relaxing but therapeutic. When my dear friend moved to Idaho I just knew our friendship would suffer. But, because of letter writing just the opposite has happened. We've grown much closer! We both find that sitting down with a cup of coffee and putting our days, thoughts and ideas (our lives!) to paper is very relaxing and connecting. It's like keeping a journal, but there's a real person on the other end. We've shared so much through the mail...hurts, sickness, raising children, joys, accomplishments and tons of laughter. Our kindred spirits have deepened and at the end of each letter I always feel a release. The best part is finding the reply within a few days. It always brightens my day. It's easier to dial the phone, but much more rewarding to send and receive a letter, a tradition that is important to maintain in our computer society. There is nothing like a handwritten letter to save and read again. It's an important tradition to pass on to our children.

Beth St. Hilaire
Harrah, WA

Sunshine & Shadows

When winter weather is getting you and your kids down, plan a picnic indoors! Pack your lunches, give each child a sack, grab your picnic quilt and march through the house until the kids are rid of some of their excess energy. Put the quilt on the floor, perhaps in front of a picture window, or in front of the fireplace...anywhere. The idea is just to change the routine mealtime and look forward to warmer temperatures and outdoor activities. My husband thought I was nuts, but everyone ended up laughing and enjoying the special time. It's been many years since my children were small, but we all still remember "winter picnics."

The new relaxation tapes or CD's help me to unwind when I become too tense. I darken the room, and only have a small lamp in the far corner. I have a candle by my chair that is always burning (it's calming, too) and then I listen to the music. My favorites are ones of thunderstorms, babbling brooks, calls of loons interspersed with pretty music. And some are simple sounds of nature. Listen, you can feel the tension leaving you.

It may sound simple, but believe me, a lot of people don't do this! If you have an appointment at a specific time, or time when you should be at work, figure out how much time you need to arrive on schedule. Then add 10 or 15 minutes. You may get caught in traffic and need that extra time, but at least you won't be late. Usually you will arrive early and have time to slow down, relax, compose yourself, and just sit for a few minutes enjoying the scenery, reading or just daydreaming. As I say, it sounds simple, but it's the simple things that are often overlooked. Your blood pressure will definitely thank you for it!

Barbara Loe
Burleson, TX

Why lose your temper, your patience, and your composure when you're stuck in traffic? Recite The Lord's Prayer...and really think about it...or meditate, or make a mental list of things you're grateful for. What a gift to everyone else in the line.

Quit thinking up excuses not to do something that needs to be done. Just do it.

Get your children to help you out of a funk. Once, when my daughter was 8, I was feeling burdened by a mountain of clothes that needed ironing. I asked her to write me a story about The Ironing Lady. This is what she wrote:

"The Ironing Lady"

Once there was a lady that loved to iron.
She ironed from morning to night.

That was the whole story, carefully printed on lined, grade-school paper. A few years later, I ran across it again and framed it. It hangs in my studio, along with another of her profound statements that was written when she was about 4. That one says "I love God." Those are two of my favorite framed works of art. They give me a boost every time I look at them.

Karyl Bannister

Talk to people. Take the time to understand them and see what they have lived through. It could help you get though a stressful time.

Megan Fryman

My way of beating the blues is to pray always and to sing and make melody in my heart to the Lord...and it works every time!

Glenda Hill
Columbus, OH

Be at peace

Exercise for me has done so many things. For one, I've fallen in love with my town. It's a great exercise area, any direction you go...it's always a workout and usually uphill. And it seems when dealing with major issues, you're more directed and relaxed and have a better inner spirit. In fact, nothing beats the strong inner spirit that you get from a good diet, exercise and fresh air.

Joann Wolfe
Sunland, CA

I put on my walking shoes, my radio head set, and have soft music playing while my dog, Barney and I walk along our Francher Creek. It's beautiful no matter what season it is...there's always something new to see. Barney is so excited...it's like he's smiling and laughing. That springer spaniel tail wags so fast and hard I can't help but laugh. By the time I get home, I feel energized and refreshed. Exercise with a good pal (Barney) does wonders for the blues.

Linda Tatman
Fresno, CA

I have enjoyed bike riding quite a bit, not only for exercise but for enjoyment, and along my way I always stop somewhere to take a rest as well as to enjoy the scenery. My favorite spot has become a bench that sits on top of a cliff facing Lake Erie. I have sat there many times and refreshed my mind while watching the sun dance on the water, and listening to the quieting sounds of nature. That feeling of calm has become a strong memory for me. Now, when I find myself caught up in a hustle-bustle situation full of stress, I close my eyes for a moment and remember the beauty of the sights and sounds, as well as the calm feeling associated with those, and it instantly brightens my outlook and lowers my heart rate! Take the time to find a special quiet spot and memorize every aspect of it. It can then become mentally soothing for you whenever you need it.

Elizabeth H. Loffredo

Pets are one of the best stress-relievers. If you own a pet, spend a few minutes with it when you get home. It can be as simple as walking the dog to the mailbox and back, but it works! Also, when you walk your dog, be sure to bring scissors and a collecting bag. If you are a crafty person, you'll be able to find a lot of stuff on your walks. I have found unusual pods, sticks and flowers that I brought home to use. Have you looked around when you walk your pet? Each walk is a new opportunity to rejoice in the natural beauty around you. It's an opportunity to meet a new friend, think things through, regroup, and become at peace within yourself.

Theresa M. Nobuyuki
Laguna Hills, CA

Two years ago I began having slightly elevated blood pressure. We also found that I was not able to take many medications to lower it. So, anything I heard, I tried. Diet, exercise, vitamins, getting a job (which I did at Gooseberry Patch). I also purchased a 30-gallon aquarium and have a dozen tropical fish. I enjoy it immensely, and my blood pressure is back down to normal. Another plus...last winter I didn't have to use the humidifier in my home. No dry, itchy skin or static shock!

Sue Major

Sunshine & Shadows

Making a list is a wonderful way to organize your daily obligations. A positive attitude can help relieve the pressure and disappointment you may feel at the end of the day when everything on your list is not crossed off. Make a new list of the things you did accomplish. Don't forget the small but important minutes spent reading to your child or telephoning a lonely friend. When everything is put into perspective, you often find that you really accomplished quite a lot...sometimes things that were much more important than those on your original "to do" list.

When things are looking bleak and I'm caught up in my own troubles, the words to an old Roger Miller song echo through my head:

"Let me be a little kinder, let me be a little blinder,
to the faults of those about me. Let me praise a little more.
Let me be when I am weary, just a little bit more cheery;
think a little more of others and little less of me."

These words always nudge me to realize that someone I know may be having a much worse day than me. I make a phone call, deliver a flower or basket of muffins, or share a hug, and somehow my own problems become manageable or even go away.

Realize that your personal stress relievers are unique for you. Learn what things revitalize and relax you and take advantage of them.

Start a collection of something you really love.

Visit a friend you haven't seen for a while.

Go somewhere you've never been.

Adopt a pet from the animal shelter.

Swimming can relax tired muscles.

Put a clock that ticks in your
most stressful room...very soothing.

Take your children strawberry or apple picking.

Learn to cat-nap...a 30 minute doze can be quite refreshing.

Turn off the telephone, television and ignore the doorbell.

Build a snowman or snow family in the front yard.

Schedule little breaks for yourself during the day.

A backrub from someone who loves you.

Comfort food (ice cream? chocolate?)...
indulge sparingly on occasion.

Roll down a grassy (or snowy) hill
with your children.

Rest on the floor while your small children
climb over you...total body massage!

Sing! Turn on a tape you love and sing while you work.

Breathe deeply.

Pray.

Mel Wolk
St. Peters, MO

*Whistle while
you work!*

Sunshine & Shadows

Tips to pamper yourself and chase away the blues:

Gathering herbs from my garden to dry by the bunches...to freeze, to make vinegars for myself and friends, and gather rose petals for sachets.

Listening to my collection of big band music of the 40's.

Enjoying things of nature...like listening to the birds sing, watching them nesting and feeding; walking among flowers, gathering them to fill the house with scent and color.

Taking off my shoes and putting my feet up.

Re-living memories which comfort me.

Reading a favorite magazine.

Being on my knees in the garden.

Sitting quietly on my patio.

Visiting antique shops.

Traveling.

Baking an apple pie.

I relax by reading poetry aloud.

Getting a professional manicure.

Breathing in the sweetness of summer air.

Visiting with my 11 year-old granddaughter.

A warm facial, a foot bath and a professional hairdo.

A meal out with family and friends at a quiet restaurant.

Enjoying my collection (over 45 years) of milk glass. Recalling the purchase of most at Westmoreland milk glass, in Pennsylvania, which was near my birthplace, but alas is no more!

Sitting, before a fireplace, looking at family albums and my Wave Navy II album.

Watching and studying the squirrels, who make my large oak tree their home.

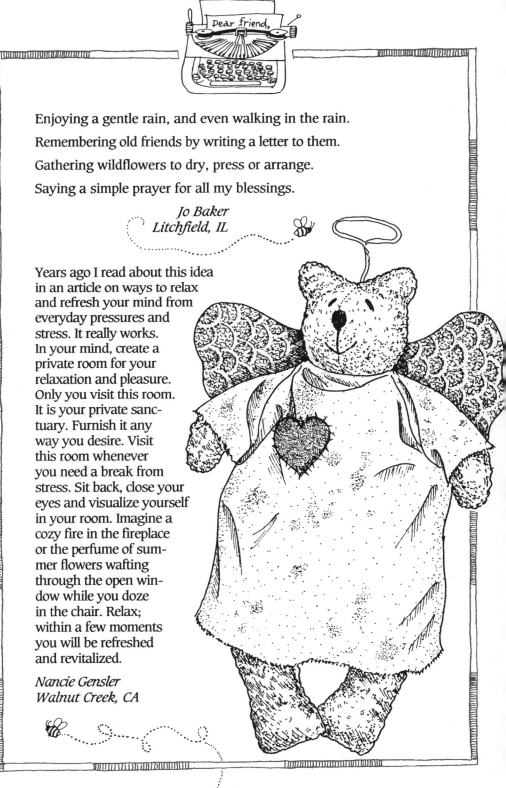

Enjoying a gentle rain, and even walking in the rain.

Remembering old friends by writing a letter to them.

Gathering wildflowers to dry, press or arrange.

Saying a simple prayer for all my blessings.

Jo Baker
Litchfield, IL

Years ago I read about this idea
in an article on ways to relax
and refresh your mind from
everyday pressures and
stress. It really works.
In your mind, create a
private room for your
relaxation and pleasure.
Only you visit this room.
It is your private sanc-
tuary. Furnish it any
way you desire. Visit
this room whenever
you need a break from
stress. Sit back, close your
eyes and visualize yourself
in your room. Imagine a
cozy fire in the fireplace
or the perfume of sum-
mer flowers wafting
through the open win-
dow while you doze
in the chair. Relax;
within a few moments
you will be refreshed
and revitalized.

Nancie Gensler
Walnut Creek, CA

Sunshine & Shadows

Just say no! We can't do everything all the time for everyone.

PRAY! This is the best stress-reliever.

Wet tea bags are great to put on your tired eyes. Helps reduce puffiness.

A paste of oatmeal and yogurt makes a great facial scrub.

One-fourth cup tomato juice and 2 tablespoons honey blended together makes a good facial mask. Apply to your face, avoid eye area, let dry, rinse off with lukewarm water. Always check to see if you are allergic to any "natural" ingredients.

Pure olive oil, warmed, makes a good hot olive hair treatment. Work about 1/4 cup olive oil into your scalp and hair, paying attention to the ends. Cover your hair with a warm damp towel for 20 minutes. Then shampoo as usual.

Sweet almond oil (from the health food store) massaged into cuticles helps soften them.

Puree two large refrigerated cucumbers into your food processor. Put the puree in a shallow pan that will accommodate your feet. Now stick your feet in and "squoosh" the cukes with your toes. Rub the puree (or better still, have your husband do it) all over your feet. Great refresher after a hard day at the mall or supermarket. Return the favor to your husband after a hard, hot day of work.

Yvonne Van Brimmer
Lompoc, CA

My garden is the perfect place to relieve stress. Who could be uptight while wandering along the flower beds pinching off spent flowers, checking out the newest day lily blossom, or sniffing the herbs? Even the sounds are relaxing. The chickadees chatter at the feeder, the trees rustle in the breeze and squirrels scamper across the yard. To me this saying is perfect for how I feel when I unwind in the garden: "One is nearer to God's heart in a garden than anywhere else on earth."

Candy Hannigan
Monument, CO

44

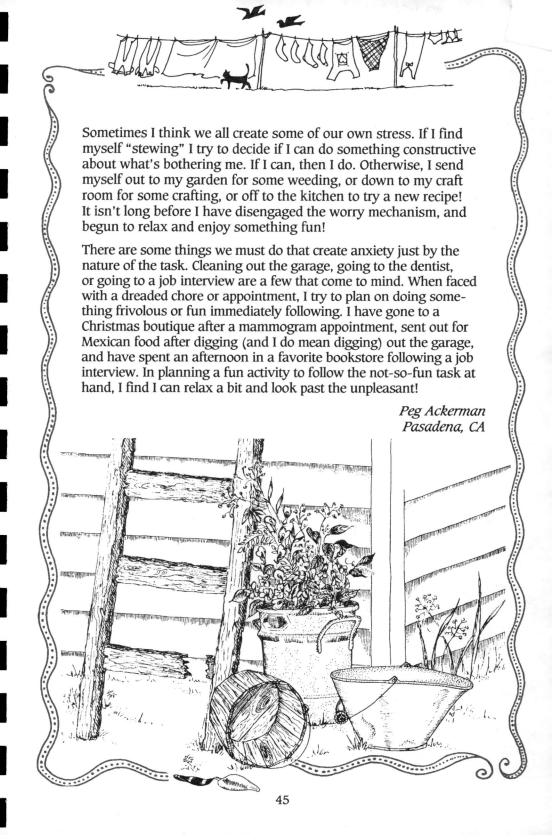

Sometimes I think we all create some of our own stress. If I find myself "stewing" I try to decide if I can do something constructive about what's bothering me. If I can, then I do. Otherwise, I send myself out to my garden for some weeding, or down to my craft room for some crafting, or off to the kitchen to try a new recipe! It isn't long before I have disengaged the worry mechanism, and begun to relax and enjoy something fun!

There are some things we must do that create anxiety just by the nature of the task. Cleaning out the garage, going to the dentist, or going to a job interview are a few that come to mind. When faced with a dreaded chore or appointment, I try to plan on doing something frivolous or fun immediately following. I have gone to a Christmas boutique after a mammogram appointment, sent out for Mexican food after digging (and I do mean digging) out the garage, and have spent an afternoon in a favorite bookstore following a job interview. In planning a fun activity to follow the not-so-fun task at hand, I find I can relax a bit and look past the unpleasant!

Peg Ackerman
Pasadena, CA

Sunshine & Shadows

When I am stressed, I have a box of Christmas fabrics handy. I go to my sewing room, play Christmas music and sew! It gets my Christmas gifts completed and I keep the Christmas spirit all year long.

Nancy Stewart
Latrobe, PA

Make the holidays less stressful by starting your Christmas shopping year 'round with your Gooseberry Patch catalogs, of course. Spreading the cost of your gifts over several months helps on the budget too!

Nancy Campbell
Bellingham, WA

Here is a tip I use when everything seems to be crashing in on me, or I just need a little time to myself. I brew a cup of tea or a special hot cocoa, sit on the porch or in a favorite chair and pull out my Gooseberry books. I don't care if it is July, and I am looking at the Christmas book or the cookie book, I just sit back and read it over. It makes me feel like I'm with a friend and sharing great ideas and recipes. It doesn't matter how many times I read the books over, I always come up with a new hint or a recipe to try on a special upcoming occasion.

Wendy Lee Paffenroth
Pine Island, NY

The public library is one of my favorite stress relievers. It's quiet, air-conditioned, comfortable and filled with books you can enjoy browsing through for hours. Many libraries have story times for children, so check it out!

Lisa Sett
Thousand Oaks, CA

Windchimes of all sizes and sounds placed strategically both inside and outside your home, along with small bird feeders, make wonderful stress reducers. There is nothing as calming as the sound of a monastic chime as you watch a bright red cardinal or brilliant yellow finch perched on a feeder.

As with most families, ours is hectic and almost constantly in motion. Our salvation is found in the half hour a day just prior to bedtime. It's then that we get calm, cuddle and connect through books. From the time my children were babies, we've observed this ritual that I know has made us stronger as a family. Every night we pick a book for each child, sit together and read. You'd be amazed at the calming effect it has, and not just on the little ones. It is also a wonderful way to encourage your young ones to read. Once that's accomplished, it's a useful tool to diagnose learning difficulties and address them before they become problems. That aside, just sitting in one place together, quietly listening or reading reminds you of what is truly important...your family.

Karen A. S. Roberts
Weymouth, MA

Spend some time with your photo albums. Everyone seems to gather 'round when the albums come out!

Sunshine & Shadows

When I was little, it always made me feel better to go swing on my swing set if I was feeling a little blue. Today I'll go to the nearby park and swing. I'm always the biggest kid on the playground!

Watch your favorite comedy movie or read a funny book. Whatever you do...laugh, laugh, laugh! It's a great way to chase those blues away.

Call a dear friend you haven't seen in a while.

Having a bad day at work? These are the days you must take a lunch break. Have lunch at a nearby park or take a walk. Do something to get out of the office. This will boost your spirits and give you the strength to face the afternoon.

I'm a firm believer in making lists to help me stay organized and to help me avoid getting stressed out. In your purse, keep a weekly list/calendar of things you need to do for your household. Before leaving work each day, make a list of what needs to be done the following day. When you come in the next day, you'll know right where to start.

I also believe that everyone needs to take a little time out for themselves. Some of my favorite ways to relax are:

On hot summer nights, I like to sit on the porch swing and listen to all the country sounds (frogs, crickets, whippoorwills). It's a great way to end a stressful day!

Sometimes I put on my straw hat and gloves and go gardening!

Or spend an hour browsing a book store.

These days everyone is so wrapped up in their work. Take time out for yourself. Pick up a new hobby such as painting, arts and crafts, etc. Let those creative juices flow.

Joy Daniel
Roland, AR

Fit for Life

Hints for cutting fat & calories (without sacrificing taste)

Okay, so you found the most delicious chocolatey cookie and it's fat-free, and cholesterol-free. That's great, but be careful! Also check the calories. Sometimes, you'll see those cookies may have 90 calories per cookie. So don't eat the whole box; those calories add up. Enjoy everything in moderation!

Lisa Sett
Thousand Oaks, CA

Do you crave chocolate? Buy a bottle of chocolate flavoring. Add 2 to 4 drops to your cup of warm milk and a little sweetener. Lo and behold, hot chocolate! And your craving is satisfied at a fraction of the calories.

Janice Parmer

Quick, low-fat snacks when you crave chocolate...small, but they get the point across:

8 oz. glass of skim milk with 1 teaspoon sugar-free cocoa mix (50 calories, 1 fat gram)

2 cream-filled chocolate sandwich cookies (100 calories, 4 fat grams)

3 chocolate candy drops (79 calories, 4 1/2 fat grams)

chocolate peppermint patty (57 calories, 1.3 fat grams)

22 plain candy-coated chocolate candies (92 calories, 4 fat grams)

1 chocolate-covered graham cracker (68 calories, 3.2 fat grams)

Cara Killingsworth
Shamrock, TX

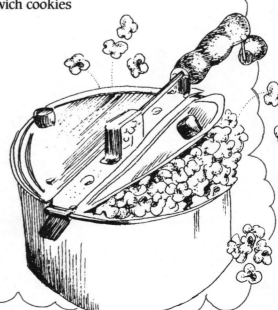

Here's a great way to fool your dieting eye. Mix French-cut green beans or any cooked julienned vegetable (such as carrots, zucchini, etc.) with your spaghetti and tomato sauce portion. It will give you the illusion of eating a whole plateful of pasta without all the calories!

Janet Marcus
Huntington, NY

Jicama is a great low-fat crunch vegetable, perfect for lunches, snacks or vegetable platters. For added variety, first slice into thin wedges, then using different shaped metal cookie cutters punch out jicama shapes.

Perri Lee McNeil
Ontario, CA

Substitute equal parts of unsweetened applesauce for vegetable oil in recipes (including boxed cakes and brownies). This creates a no-fat alternative to the oil, and enhances the moisture of the product.

Marinate chicken breasts, pork or beef in low-fat Italian salad dressing overnight. Grill or broil to your liking. What a great flavor!

Raisins are great "add-ins." Raisins are rich in carbohydrates, fiber, iron and potassium. They contain no fat or cholesterol and are guilt-free.

Susan Harvey
Red Lion, PA

Some crunchy, and satisfying low-fat foods:
Air-popped or pan-popped seasoned popcorn
Graham crackers
Bread sticks
Pretzels
Apples
Rice cakes
Baby carrots
Bagels with jam
Oven-baked potato chips
Cereals (check labels!), dry or with skim milk

Fit for Life

Use chicken broth instead of oil to sauté or stir-fry. When opening a can of chicken broth, remove any fat from surface, use what you need, and pour the extra into ice cube trays and freeze. The next time you need a little broth, pop out a cube and place it in your frying pan.

Use evaporated skim milk instead of cream in sauces.

Try spreading your bagel with fat-free cream cheese. A bagel has only one gram of fat.

For toast, start with light bread with one gram fat for two slices of bread. Instead of spreading with butter or margarine, spread with light preserves (no fat and fewer calories.)

Almost any recipe can be modified by substituting fat-free or low-fat products as ingredients. The challenge keeps you going.

Use butter-flavored mix or liquid in place of oil and butter...zero fat.

Janice Ertola
Martinez, CA

Healthy Recipe Substitutions

Instead of:	Use:
1 c. butter or solid shortening	1 c. margarine or 3/4 c. vegetable oil
1 c. sour cream	1 c. low-fat plain yogurt 1 cup low-fat cottage cheese, blended or 1 c. low-fat ricotta cheese
1 egg, whole	1/4 c. egg substitute or 2 egg whites or 1 egg white plus 1 t. vegetable oil
2 whole eggs	2 egg whites plus one whole egg
1 oz. baking chocolate	3 T. cocoa plus 1 T. vegetable oil

Mel Wolk
St. Peters, MO

Since I love to eat volumes of food, diets never really worked for me (long term, that is). So I began with shopping healthy...low-fat and fat-free. I didn't concern myself too much with low sugar. So, I made breakfast and lunch fat-free! I ate cereal, fruit, fat-free bread and bagels. Then, I'd eat a sensible dinner and always have fat-free dressing on my salad. Without starving, I dropped 12 pounds! No kidding...I was shocked! I wish I'd known this years ago...it would have saved many tears! Some ideas that I have used are:

When I go out to dinner, I bring my own fat-free salad dressing and fat-free mayonnaise. That way, if I go to a salad bar, I load up on fresh veggies and lettuce and go away with no guilt. If I order a sandwich, I have my own mayo, too.

If I go out to breakfast, I bring my own fat-free cream cheese to use on a bagel or English muffin.

I carry fat-free granola bars and fat-free pretzels with me if I'm going to be out and may not have lunch at my regular time...a "snack" gets me through without fat.

I always keep fat-free chicken broth on hand for all sorts of cooking...adds great flavor to mashed potatoes, and is great for basting turkey breast.

I use low-fat margarine for lots of cooking...can be rubbed on turkey breast under skin and all over, then pour fat-free chicken broth over breast and cook according to size of breast. Outstanding!

For those who must have butter in mashed potatoes, add low-fat margarine instead.

For low-fat, stove-prepared stuffing, do not add butter or water...replace amount of water with fat-free chicken broth and omit butter.

Angie Yanchik
Cherry Hill, NJ

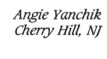

Vegetable/Relish Centerpieces

I like to assemble a relish/vegetable centerpiece using a styrofoam cone in the middle of a tray. The cones come in several sizes, can be used several times, and are readily available in craft stores.

Cover the styrofoam with large lettuce leaves, letting the ruffled edges show. Secure the lettuce to the cone with regular wooden toothpicks.

I like to use cubes of cheese, rolled wafer-sliced ham, ripe and green olives, chunks of celery, pearl onions, thinly sliced carrots, midget sweet pickles, radish roses...the list goes on and on. Layer 2 or 3 of the above on a pretty cello-tipped toothpick and stick into the cone. Cover the cone and you will be surprised!!

You may want to anchor the cone with double-faced tape to the platter. Alternately place slices of ripe tomato, Vidalia (sweet) onions, and green peppers around the cone on the platter. In the summer, I also like to use deviled eggs.

You can use any vegetable of your choice, taking advantage of the season and your garden. These relish trays are delicious and very "showy" at picnics and church dinners. But the best part is that this is a family activity. All ages have fun helping assemble the "trees."

Lydia Hall
Cordell, OK

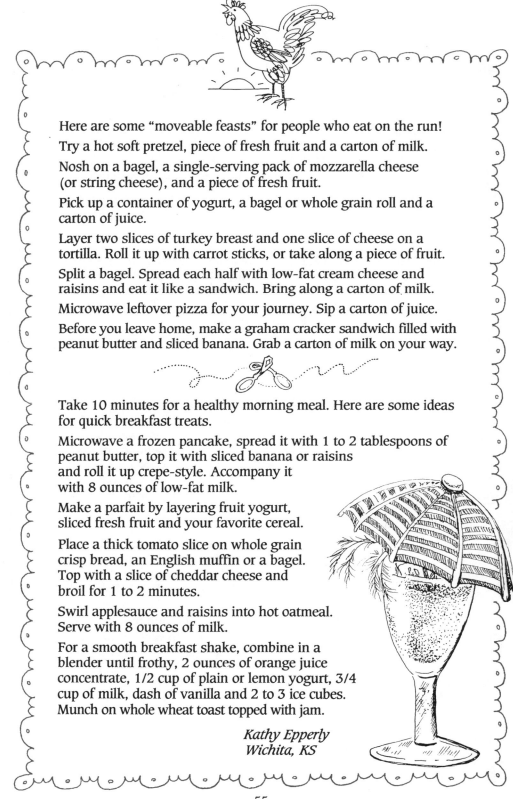

Here are some "moveable feasts" for people who eat on the run!

Try a hot soft pretzel, piece of fresh fruit and a carton of milk.

Nosh on a bagel, a single-serving pack of mozzarella cheese (or string cheese), and a piece of fresh fruit.

Pick up a container of yogurt, a bagel or whole grain roll and a carton of juice.

Layer two slices of turkey breast and one slice of cheese on a tortilla. Roll it up with carrot sticks, or take along a piece of fruit.

Split a bagel. Spread each half with low-fat cream cheese and raisins and eat it like a sandwich. Bring along a carton of milk.

Microwave leftover pizza for your journey. Sip a carton of juice.

Before you leave home, make a graham cracker sandwich filled with peanut butter and sliced banana. Grab a carton of milk on your way.

Take 10 minutes for a healthy morning meal. Here are some ideas for quick breakfast treats.

Microwave a frozen pancake, spread it with 1 to 2 tablespoons of peanut butter, top it with sliced banana or raisins and roll it up crepe-style. Accompany it with 8 ounces of low-fat milk.

Make a parfait by layering fruit yogurt, sliced fresh fruit and your favorite cereal.

Place a thick tomato slice on whole grain crisp bread, an English muffin or a bagel. Top with a slice of cheddar cheese and broil for 1 to 2 minutes.

Swirl applesauce and raisins into hot oatmeal. Serve with 8 ounces of milk.

For a smooth breakfast shake, combine in a blender until frothy, 2 ounces of orange juice concentrate, 1/2 cup of plain or lemon yogurt, 3/4 cup of milk, dash of vanilla and 2 to 3 ice cubes. Munch on whole wheat toast topped with jam.

Kathy Epperly
Wichita, KS

Do not pour extra calories on your salad. Instead, order your dressing on the side and before each bite, dip your fork tines into the dressing and then into your salad. This way, with every bite you get a taste of dressing. You will be amazed at how little dressing you will use.

Marie Alana Gardner
North Tonawanda, NY

Water! Water! Water! It's a great way to lose weight, and it's so good for you. Drink a full glass before meals, it helps you feel full so you'll eat less. Fill a sports bottle up and take it with you wherever you go...out gardening, in the car, to work. Add a slice of orange, lemon or lime or a sprig of mint. It's so refreshing!

Kimberly Smeets
Sherwood, OR

Do you often eat fast food high in fat because you lack the time and energy to fix a "healthy meal?" Take one weekend to fix a bunch of healthy casseroles and dinners to put in your freezer for future use.

Keep vegetables and chicken already cut up in your freezer. Perfect for a quick and easy stir-fry. Make a double batch when you cook. Eat one casserole tonight, and put the other in the freezer for future use.

Joy Daniel
Roland, AR

These days it's easy to find a variety of low-fat and no-fat items in the grocery store. Even the all-time fatty favorites like chocolate fudge ice cream, potato chips, coffee cake, hot dogs, cookies, crackers, dips, sauces, and cheeses come in a no-fat version!

One tasty discovery I made was to eliminate all mayonnaise (100% fat) in my diet and replace it with a no-fat, creamy ranch salad dressing. Use the salad dressing just as you would mayonnaise. It's delicious used as a sandwich spread in tuna and chicken salads, as well as garden salads!

When cooking ground beef for casseroles, spaghetti sauce, etc., buy the leanest beef possible. Use a non-stick frying pan and do not add any oil. After browning, pour beef into a colander and rinse it off with water.This will eliminate most of the remaining fat.

Linda Lee
Tucker, GA

While working in the kitchen, keep a tall glass of ice water close by to sip. This will curb your appetite and make you less likely to nibble. Add a slice of lemon to make it taste great!

Karen Wald
Dalton, OH

Sing in the shower!

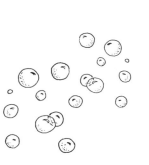

Store canned soups in the fridge. When ready to use, simply open and skim the fat off the contents for a healthy meal. The taste is not altered, and you don't miss the grease. The same method is used to remove grease from beef. Chill the broth. When cold, just spoon the hard fat from the juice and prepare the stew, noodles or whatever you desire.

Phyllis Peters
Three Rivers, MI

Think about becoming healthier and more fit, rather than just being thin. There are lots of thin, unhealthy people and very fit larger people. Fat is not healthy, but starvation is an unhealthy way to achieve thinness.

Use fruit juice concentrate, applesauce, prune puree or cooked, pureed sweet potato as an oil substitute in breads, cakes, biscuits and muffins.

In mashed potatoes, use a tablespoon of ranch dressing mix (dry) or butter-flavored sprinkles.

Don't stir-fry in oil; use fat-free vegetarian broth powder in a little water.

Most beans and legumes (except garbanzos) are fat-free. Use fat-free vegetarian broth powder, herbs and spices instead of lard, bacon and pork fat for seasoning. Beans added to salads are fat-free, but not calorie free. They contain lots of fiber, so they help to lower cholesterol too.

Using ground beef with 8% fat may be more expensive, but there's hardly any waste and much fewer fat calories than 25% to 30% in hamburger.

In most cakes, muffins, quick breads, brownies, biscuits and scones you can substitute, measure for measure, the fat with:

pureed fruit   applesauce
fruit juice or concentrate   prune butter
mashed pumpkin or squash   non-fat yogurt
buttermilk

Follow the food pyramid plan and it's hard to eat too much. This hint came from one of my college nutrition teachers.

Yvonne Van Brimmer
Lompoc, CA

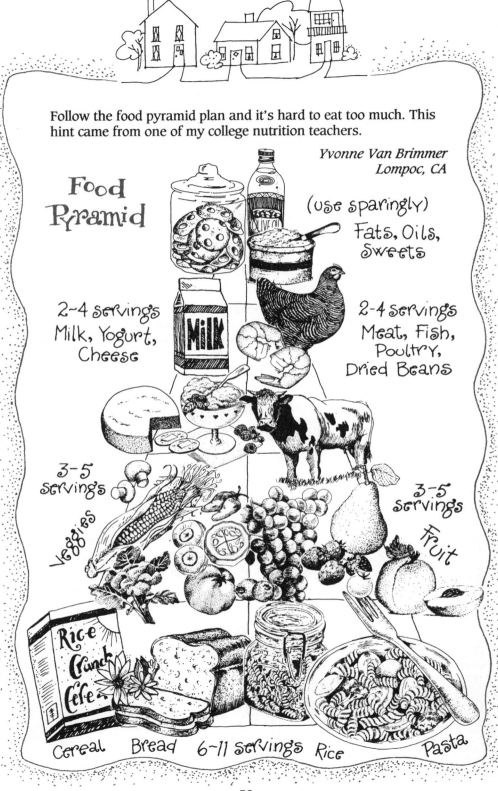

Food Pyramid

(use sparingly)
Fats, Oils, Sweets

2-4 servings
Milk, Yogurt, Cheese

2-4 servings
Meat, Fish, Poultry, Dried Beans

3-5 servings
Veggies

3-5 servings
Fruit

Cereal   Bread   6-11 servings   Rice   Pasta

Fit for Life

Whenever possible, use cocoa for flavoring instead of melted chocolate. This gives the flavor of chocolate without the fat. Then you can modify the amount of oil or other added fat to achieve a healthier product.

Use two egg whites instead of one whole egg. The white contains the protein, while the fat is in the yolk.

Use vegetable spray and nonstick pans when pan "frying." You can eliminate most or all of the oil, margarine or other fat called for in recipes by doing this.

You can de-fat broths or soups by dropping in an ice cube. The fat will collect on the cube; then you can dip it out and discard it.

Use sharp or extra-sharp when cheese is called for in a recipe. You can use less cheese (which is high in fat) without decreasing your flavor. You could also substitute half non-fat or reduced fat cheese with half sharp for the amount of cheese called for.

Chop your chocolate chips into smaller bits and use half as much. The smaller pieces will go further and you will cut your fat in half. One bag of semi-sweet chips is about 1600 calories, half of that from fat!

Replace whole milk with low-fat or non-fat (skim) milk.

Replace cream with evaporated skim milk. This saves about 500 calories for each cup replaced.

Whenever you modify your recipes, try changing one ingredient at a time. This way you will know what is wrong if the recipe doesn't turn out. Also, keep quiet about the recipe being low-fat until everyone has tried it. For some reason, many people think healthy food won't taste as good!

Cheryl N. Berry
Gainesville, FL

Cream cheese is the most often used dip base, but two 3-ounce packages of cream cheese and 4 tablespoons of milk add to a cupful of dip base that's 680 calories, or 43 calories a tablespoon! Create a lighter base...mock cream cheese. Use one 8-ounce container of part-skim ricotta. It's only 320 calories a cupful, or 20 calories per tablespoon.

Mary K. Murray
Mount Vernon, OH

The average American consumes 128 pounds of refined sugar each year.

How to substitute for refined sugar in recipes:

Honey: 1/2 to 3/4 cup honey for each cup of sugar in most recipes. Reduce liquid in recipe by 1/4 cup for each cup of honey substituted.

Molasses: 1/2 cup to 3/4 cup molasses for each cup of honey in most recipes. Reduce liquid in recipe by 1/4 cup for each cup of honey substituted. Add 1/4 teaspoon baking soda per 1/2 cup molasses used.

Mel Wolk,
St. Peters, MO

When bananas are just too far gone, stash them, peel and all, in the freezer. Put them in a plastic bag, one by one, as they accumulate. When you need them for muffins, bread, etc. just take them out and peel them. They'll be fine, and you don't have to make that banana bread when you don't feel like it. Don't be a slave to anything... especially bananas! Toss frozen (peeled) chunks of banana into a blender with milk and a couple of drops of vanilla to make a swell, thick shake. Can also be flavored with some orange or apple juice. The frozen banana makes it thick, so don't defrost it first.

Karyl Bannister

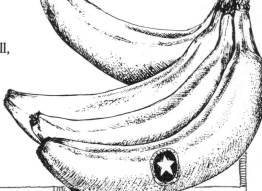

I have substituted 2 egg whites for each whole egg for 12 years now. You just cannot tell the difference. I cannot eat the yolks because they make me ill, but who wants the cholesterol and fat anyway? No one ever notices the difference. You can add 1 teaspoon canola oil for each 2 egg whites if you want to, in baked goods or meatloaf. It isn't necessary to purchase egg substitutes; they are made the same way; they just add yellow food coloring, and the yolks go down the drain. Some people put them on their plants but I find this too messy and it can have an unpleasant odor. "Tossing" the egg yolks doesn't break my food budget, and you save by not purchasing the egg substitutes.

Barbara Loe
Burleson, TX

Grow or buy sprouts (we love alfalfa sprouts) to top off sandwiches or add crunch to salads.

When preparing pasta salad use spinach and/or tomato pastas.

Save celery leaves when cleaning celery: wash, dry, and use in soups. It's easy to cut back on calories when fresh vegetables and fruits are in season...eat them raw and unadorned!

Spice up your applesauce with cinnamon, nutmeg, and/or vanilla instead of sugar... I never use sugar when preparing applesauce for canning. Combine golden delicious apples with other varieties, or use solely for your sauce. They are so sweet without adding sugar. You can add the cinnamon, nutmeg, or vanilla while preparing sauce, or just before serving.

Judy Hand
Centre Hall, PA

Help!
I want to lose a few pounds!

Great ideas for motivation & reward

Help!
I want to lose a few pounds!

To reduce your weight, keep your fat intake at 20 to 30 grams of fat per day. Drink 8 or more glasses of water per day. Get an aerobic workout...35 to 45 minutes at least 3 times per week.

Janice Ertola
Martinez, CA

Lose weight for yourself, not to please someone else.

A hint to losing weight: Use a smaller plate with regular food. Used consistently, your pounds will diminish. It may take longer to get to your goal, but the excess pounds will stay off, and you won't feel deprived.

Nancy Campbell
Bellingham, WA

Today, many of us strive to make long-lasting, healthful changes to our lifestyles. Most often, these include exercise and diet. To keep from getting overwhelmed by these alterations, I prioritize the changes I want to make and tackle them one at a time. Keep it simple!! When I have had a success with one, I move to the next. After trying new behaviors in what I call "do-able doses," I am more pleased with what's been accomplished and less upset if there are smaller defeats. It's a wonderful feeling to cross something off my list of priorities and then add new things, too!!

PS: My priority this summer was to begin a walking program. After two months, I'm now walking between 15 to 20 miles a week and feeling GREAT!

Christine Mattox
Tucker, GA

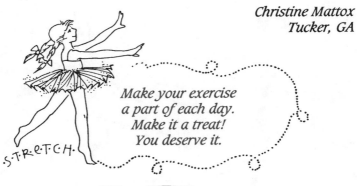

Make your exercise
a part of each day.
Make it a treat!
You deserve it.

S·T·R·e·T·C·H·

If you are discouraged watching exercise videos filled with gorgeous, thin models, rent one of Richard Simmons' "Sweating to the Oldies." These videos are filled with regular people, all ages, sizes, men and women...plus great music.

Have a snack area in your fridge and pantry so everyone will be able to help themselves and not accidentally eat something needed for dinner or special recipes.

Lisa Sett
Thousand Oaks, CA

My son is a physician, and he tells his patients to try to exercise as often as possible. I try to walk at least four or five times a week.

You can replace fat-laden foods with fresh fruits and vegetables, grainy brown breads, pastas and potatoes topped with fat-free cheese and spicy sauces. You can have treats such as angel food cake, fresh berries, frozen yogurt, fat-free cookies, pretzels and even a few gum drops. It's never too late to change and experience a healthy new lifestyle.

Begin a moderate walking program and cut the fat. Don't overeat on the fat-free desserts. Keeping a food journal helps. Make sure you get enough protein.

Judy Borecky
Escondido, CA

Help!
I want to lose a few pounds!

If you want to determine how much "extra weight" you are carrying around each day, save a couple of plastic milk gallon containers, fill them with water and replace caps. One filled container weighs about 8 pounds. You may need to lose only one container worth of weight, or you may need to line up several containers. When you can actually see and feel all this extra weight, you will be inspired to lose it! As you gradually shed a pound or two each week, pour off that much of your "water weight" from one of your gallon containers. This is a great motivation, as you virtually watch your weight disappear down the drain!

Forget dieting and counting calories! In order to lose weight and keep it off, you must do two things: reduce the amount of fat in your diet and increase your physical activity. Find a good diet book that stresses the relationship between low-fat eating and weight loss. Most of these books will have a fat-gram chart in them. Be honest with yourself and find the "hidden" fat in your current diet. Resolve to eliminate these foods, or find tasty, low-fat substitutes for them. If you have never been active before, try walking! It's great exercise, easy and cheap! The more you exercise and maintain a low-fat diet, the quicker you will lose weight. Eat when you are hungry, eat until you are satisfied. Just make sure you are eating low-fat or no-fat foods. Study your fat gram chart! Read all food labels for fat grams per serving. Remember, most people eat more than the typical per-serving size. Pretty soon these changes in your eating and exercising habits will become natural. Because you will never be hungry, you will not feel deprived. You will never lose control, go on "binges," and feel guilty afterwards. Most importantly, you will not become obsessed with food or counting calories. As you watch the pounds melt away, you will become more motivated and determined to continue. This is not a "diet" you go on and off, this is simply a positive lifestyle change that you can live with!

Linda Lee
Tucker, GA

Exercise can be the most difficult thing in the world to get started (I know from experience). One thing to remember is that it takes 21 days to form a habit. So, if for 21 days you faithfully exercise every day for at least 15 minutes, you will have formed a good habit of exercising. Once exercise becomes a part of your every-day routine, you will begin to feel better, look better, and have more energy.

All of us are tempted to eat that last big slice of homemade apple pie left in the fridge. I have found in the past that the temptation... well, you've probably been there; you know. I have found that leaving a little note on my fridge that says, "Remember to eat healthy and wise, than eat those fat-filled pies," helps me curb that temptation.

When you are craving the taste of a double chocolate, chocolate chip chocolate cake, don't deny yourself; simply cut yourself a tiny slice of cake. It will curb your craving, and you won't feel so bad.

As a good rule of thumb, always go to the grocery store on a full tummy; that way you won't over-spend or buy a bunch of junk food.

Crystal Parker
Gooseberry Patch Group Leader

I'd rather quilt or sew or garden than exercise, so I never seem to find the time to do it. A friend and I meet once a week (well, that is better than nothing!) at a local mall an hour before we have to be at work. We spend 30 to 40 minutes walking in the temperature-controlled, well-lit, almost empty mall while catching up on each other's news...instead of doing it on the phone. The time flies, and I never even think of it as exercise. Sometimes she pushes her two little girls in the double stroller and she gets an even better workout...especially going up the sloped areas.

Candy Hannigan
Monument, CO

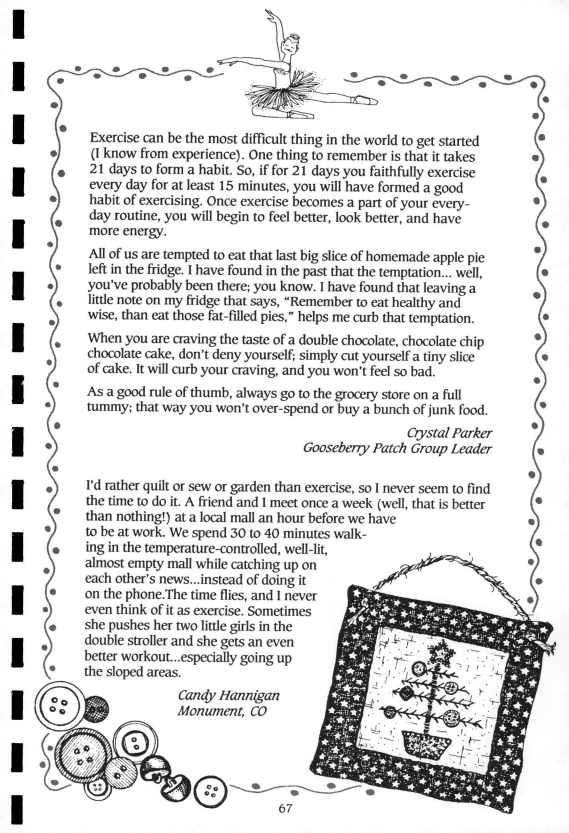

Help!
I want to lose a few pounds!

As I am an overweight diabetic, I have become very aware that what I eat affects my health. Under the supervision of my doctor, using a controlled diet, I have slowly lost 23 pounds in the past year. Finding myself at a standstill in weight reduction, I persevered; 4 more pounds came off these past two months, by eliminating sweets and consuming only about 1/4 of my daily calories in fat. I use a minimum of salt. Herbs from my garden are used extensively. I have found a healthier way of eating. I consume lots of fruits and vegetables; which help me generate and use energy. There is a whole variety of foods in our markets today which lend themselves to weight reduction and diabetics. I have become an avid label reader. Exercise and attitude are very important in a diet. You must stick to your diet. I learned the hard way. The following are food groups you should incorporate into your diet each day: starches, lean meats, vegetables, fruits, low-fat milk and small amounts of unsaturated fats.

Jo Baker
Litchfield, IL

Consider becoming a vegetarian. Include a vegetarian dish in your menu two or three times a week. Purchase a vegetarian cookbook, especially one with international dishes, and experiment with unfamiliar spices, condiments, beans and grain. You'll be amazed at how tasty meatless meals can be.

Nancie Gensler
Walnut Creek, CA

You've been great all week...watching your fat intake, a little exercise and you feel great. So buy yourself a little treat. Instead of that candy bar, buy a new book or a bunch of flowers or a new nightie. Later, you'll be glad that you did!

Deb Weiser
Gooseberry Patch Warehouse

Park as far away as possible when at a mall or the grocery store. The extra walking will burn extra calories. Also take the stairs instead of the elevator for another simple, but healthy, lifestyle change.

Judy Gidley
Greenville, NC

Get in the habit of brushing your teeth immediately after a meal. When your mouth tastes fresh and clean, you are less tempted to pick at leftovers or eat dessert. This tip also works well for people trying to quit smoking cigarettes.

Gina Moretti
Santa Ysabel, CA

I try to hang my laundry outside as much as possible, weather permitting, all year 'round. Try to hang the line high enough, so you must really reach overhead. This is great outside exercise, and did you ever notice how long music conductors live?

Debbie Benjamin

Recipe Organizer

Sharon Chelin
Sandy, OR

I had a folder full of low-calorie, low-fat recipes I had cut out of magazines, newspapers, cookbooks, and copied from friends and family. But I was always digging through them to find a favorite one, or would lose a favorite one. I found an easy solution. Here's all you'll need:

2 loose-leaf binders
100 top-loading clear sheet protectors
Pkg. 8 1/2" x 11" constuction paper
glue stick

Lightly glue recipes to the colored paper, picking one color for each category. After a page is full, slip the recipe page into the top loading sheet protector and put it in the binder. A color-coded card in front of the binder will help you find the different categories, for example...bright blue for soups, hot pink for beef, yellow for chicken, green for fish, purple for pork. A second binder would have vegetables, salads, desserts, drinks, etc.

The pages are washable, and if you find you have included a recipe you don't like, just slip the paper out of the sheet protector, carefully lift the recipe off the colored paper, and glue another recipe in its place. I have even made up a binder with articles on weight loss ideas, exercise ideas, ways to lead a healthier life, etc. No more digging through my magazines to find that article I read that was so helpful and full of ideas!

Make a list of five reasons you want to lose weight. Recite them to yourself first thing in the morning and whenever you go to reach for that piece of fudge cake. You might even want to post them on the fridge as a reminder throughout the day!

Munchies & More

Fun & easy recipes & ideas that are good for kids

LemonAid
20¢

Browniez
25¢

Munchies & More

Remember to enjoy your children every day by listening to them. You may be surprised at what you hear.

Mary Ann Nemecek
Springfield, IL

Have children plant fast-growing garden cress. Planting this herb gives a child an instant feeling of success. Have the child "write" his or her name in cress seed. Water it and watch it grow!

Kids love to write secret notes. This is a trick I learned as a nanny. Little boys love to pretend they are spies. Write the message on paper with lemon juice or milk with a stick or a toothpick. When it dries, the words are invisible. To read the message, press the paper with a warm iron. The words come back like magic!

If you have lots of kids, lots of bubbles, but not enough bubble pipes...improvise! Use red trumpet flowers. Pull out the stamen to create a little hole, pinch the hole closed, pour in a small amount of bubble mixture, tilt the blossom up and blow from the wide part of petals. Never another argument over the bubble pipes or wands again!

Take the kids to the beach for sailing without even leaving home! Make walnut sailboats from halved walnut hulls filled with a bit of glue, mud or even a gumdrop...which works great! Use a twig, toothpick or matchstick for the mast. Use a leaf or a piece of paper for the sail. Sail these magnificent sailing vessels in a big puddle, a rain-swollen gutter or even a big bucket. This will delight kids and adults as well!

Jeannine English
Wylie, TX

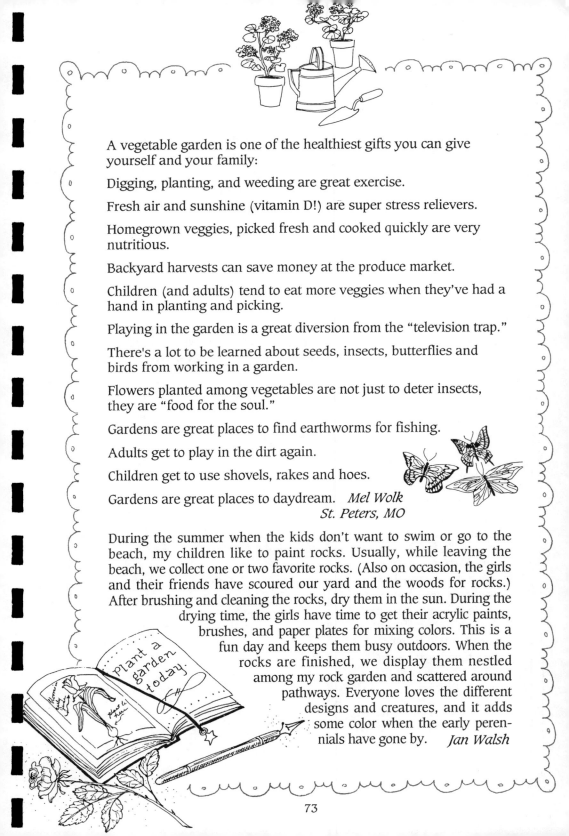

A vegetable garden is one of the healthiest gifts you can give yourself and your family:

Digging, planting, and weeding are great exercise.

Fresh air and sunshine (vitamin D!) are super stress relievers.

Homegrown veggies, picked fresh and cooked quickly are very nutritious.

Backyard harvests can save money at the produce market.

Children (and adults) tend to eat more veggies when they've had a hand in planting and picking.

Playing in the garden is a great diversion from the "television trap."

There's a lot to be learned about seeds, insects, butterflies and birds from working in a garden.

Flowers planted among vegetables are not just to deter insects, they are "food for the soul."

Gardens are great places to find earthworms for fishing.

Adults get to play in the dirt again.

Children get to use shovels, rakes and hoes.

Gardens are great places to daydream.   *Mel Wolk*
                                                St. Peters, MO

During the summer when the kids don't want to swim or go to the beach, my children like to paint rocks. Usually, while leaving the beach, we collect one or two favorite rocks. (Also on occasion, the girls and their friends have scoured our yard and the woods for rocks.) After brushing and cleaning the rocks, dry them in the sun. During the drying time, the girls have time to get their acrylic paints, brushes, and paper plates for mixing colors. This is a fun day and keeps them busy outdoors. When the rocks are finished, we display them nestled among my rock garden and scattered around pathways. Everyone loves the different designs and creatures, and it adds some color when the early perennials have gone by.   *Jan Walsh*

Take a small child to the zoo. It's great seeing the animals through a child's excited eyes!

Put out the play clay and finger paints and create some wonderful works of art with your children. You'll be spending some quality time with your kids and, at the same time, forgetting all your troubles (at least for a little while).

Take your kids to visit a pumpkin patch in the fall!

Joy Daniel
Roland, AR

When planning a trip to the beach, lake or any picnic, freeze six or more juice boxes the night before. When packing the cooler, place each frozen juice box in a sandwich bag (they sweat when they thaw) and place around the food to keep it cold. Drink at the end of the day when they are thawed and still cold, or let the kids drink them when they turn to slush.

Wendy Lee Paffenroth
Pine Island, NY

Always carry a wet wash cloth sealed in a plastic bag. It can come in handy at picnics, ball games, school trips, camping, etc. It can be used to cool someone down, or to clean a cut or scrape. Also, if the wash cloth is red, it will help conceal blood from a child who gets upset at the sight of blood.

Mary Ann Nemecek
Springfield, IL

For summer, when the kids are playing outside, I take an insulated jug and fill it with lots of ice and water and set it outside on the picnic table with some cups. When the kids are thirsty, they can get their own water and they aren't tramping through the house for something to drink.

Also, when we travel, we let the kids take a sports bottle full of ice water and a few healthy snacks (fruit, crackers, etc.). Then when we make our bathroom stops, they aren't always asking us to buy pop and snacks at the rest stops.

We always keep a plastic pitcher of ice water in the refrigerator so that the kids can get their own. It tastes so much better than plain tap water.

Here's an idea for a way to get your kids to eat fruit while staying at a hotel on vacation. This summer our friends couldn't make it on vacation with us as they always had before. We were pleasantly surprised on the first day at the hotel when we walked into our room and found a fruit basket from them. We bought a foam cooler, put the fruit on ice that needed to be, bought a paring knife and some small plates and napkins, and had fresh fruit in the morning before we went out. We also bought bottled water and put it on ice. The kids drank that when thirsty instead of pop.

Next year, we may send ourselves a fruit basket (you could write a great message to the kids on the card) and the plates, napkins and knife. That way, the kids won't have to go to the grocery store and miss any beach time. The local convenience store will provide the cooler and bottled water.

Don't forget to take everyone's vitamins with you on vacation. With all the activities, it's sometimes hard to eat three good meals a day.

Susan Kornowki
Duncansville, PA

Build a sandcastle.

Munchies & More

Sometimes, in the fall, the winds get so strong that we lose our electricity service for hours (sometimes a day or two!). Of course, living in earthquake country, we have the flashlights ready to go, and if we have to cook, we have the propane barbecue. The challenge, though, is having to find alternative activities that don't require power. No TV, VCR, CD player, video games or other amusements. What a great opportunity to play a board game, card game or to do a craft together as a family! (What a concept!) We have pulled out candles and played board games by candlelight. We have told ghost stories while sitting in front of the fireplace. We even do "s'mores" in the fireplace. A perfect time to regroup as a family!

I remember going away to camp as a kid, and loving every minute of it. Being the eldest of six, I guess my parents thought it would be a nice change for me! One of the things I remember about camp is the campfire. We'd sing, have skits, and then, at the end of the evening, everyone would hold hands, making a friendship circle (sometimes two or three, depending on how many kids were at the campfire). We would softly sing taps, and then... silence. The camp director would gently squeeze the hand of the girl next to her, and the friendship squeeze would continue until everyone had passed it on. Then, quietly, the girls would leave the campfire without talking (well, almost no talking) and return to their camp areas. A wonderful way to wrap up a busy day at camp!

Peg Ackerman
Pasadena, CA

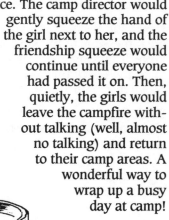

I purchased pumpkin carving knives for my children so that they can help cut up things in the kitchen without the danger of getting cut. These knives are not sharp, and the kids love helping!

Renee Hobler

On warm summer nights, we love to take out sleeping bags and open them up so all four of us can lie under the stars and talk. It's relaxing, thought-provoking, and fun. We bring out snacks and juice and have a night-time picnic. It's especially exciting on nights we are having meteor showers. The stars and falling bright meteors are awesome!!

The Walsh Family
Hingham, MA

When my daughter went off to kindergarten at age 5 (she's now 13!) I started a special tradition. Each day I'd put a note on her napkin. Maybe it was a heart, a star, an "XO", an angel, a balloon, an "I love you," a "See you after school" or "There's a surprise at home!" As her reading improved, the messages developed into notes. She always looked forward to these...a little extra security from home. It always surprised me that few of the other children had messages from home. Sometimes we get so busy that we forget the little things that mean so much.

Beth St. Hilaire
Harrah, WA

Tradition...stuff you can count on! Whatever you choose, do it at the same time, every year, the same way. Your children will love it!

Have each of your children pick a veggie to plant and tend and harvest in your garden. Saves money and time, and encourages organic gardening and eating good foods.

For home schooling families, the exercise of a family walk can be a learning experience. You can observe birds, leaves, types of cars, homes, geometric shapes, etc. Take a notebook to record finds, a bag for samples or a camera for special pictures.

Make a "food pyramid" for each child and let them find the corresponding foods in magazines to place in the pyramid.

Only keep good healthy snacks around. Good ones are pretzels, baked tortilla chips, whole-grain crackers, cut-up fruit, ready-to-eat vegetables, fat-free yogurt, granola, and low-fat granola bars or cookies.

Be a good example. Don't eat a gooey candy bar, then tell your children to eat carrot sticks!

Any child over the age or 2 or 3 can learn to drink skim milk.

Make healthy food fun. Use a garnishing tool, crinkle cutter and spiral slicer to prepare fruits and vegetables. Whole-grain cracker recipes can be cut with fun cookie cutters. Whole-grain breads can be cut with cookie cutters too.

Yvonne Van Brimmer
Lompoc, CA

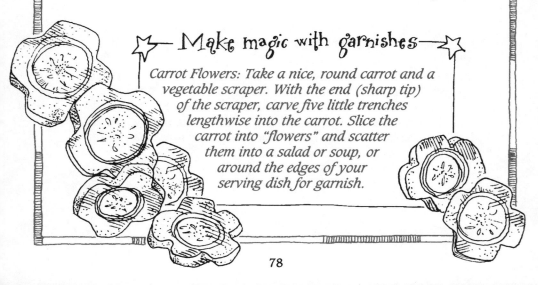

✫ Make magic with garnishes ✫

Carrot Flowers: Take a nice, round carrot and a vegetable scraper. With the end (sharp tip) of the scraper, carve five little trenches lengthwise into the carrot. Slice the carrot into "flowers" and scatter them into a salad or soup, or around the edges of your serving dish for garnish.

Bedtime for my children has never been much of a struggle. I entice them with a night time routine that includes one-on-one attention with games, gabbing and giggles! After bedtime stories, each child gets a gentle "1-2-3" toss into bed and then a series of short games that vary according to mood. We lay on opposite ends of the bed and pull each other up for "see-saw," mirror each other's funny faces, check tickle spots (to see if they're working), and end with a spelling or math game that gets a tickle or back scratch for every correct answer. And, of course, lots of kisses and hugs.

Louise Montillio

A good way to "stop and smell the roses" is to let someone know you love them. My young daughter and I sometimes walk hand in hand through the park, and I tell her I love her. Sometimes people can forget to tell their children this. It becomes something that people take for granted, or they find it difficult to say. But it means so much to a child.

Deberah Green

Share the love of reading with your children. Go to the library and choose a book the whole family will enjoy. Read aloud to them.

Take your grandchildren camping, one at a time. They have your undivided attention, and you can see things with their eyes. Make special memories for both of you. Take snapshots, too!

Sing, sing, sing! My children and grandchildren know all of my old camp, school and Girl Scout songs. We just don't get enough spontaneous singing anymore.

Nancy Campbell
Bellingham, WA

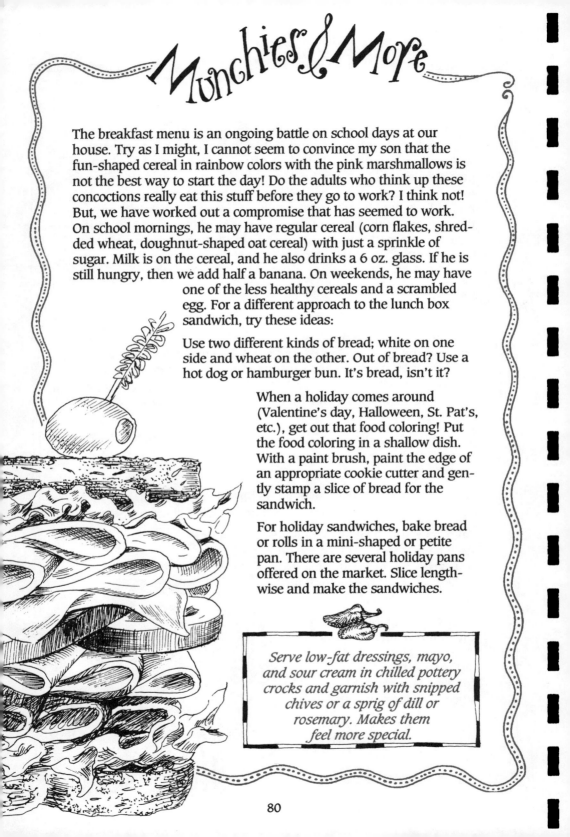

Munchies & More

The breakfast menu is an ongoing battle on school days at our house. Try as I might, I cannot seem to convince my son that the fun-shaped cereal in rainbow colors with the pink marshmallows is not the best way to start the day! Do the adults who think up these concoctions really eat this stuff before they go to work? I think not! But, we have worked out a compromise that has seemed to work. On school mornings, he may have regular cereal (corn flakes, shredded wheat, doughnut-shaped oat cereal) with just a sprinkle of sugar. Milk is on the cereal, and he also drinks a 6 oz. glass. If he is still hungry, then we add half a banana. On weekends, he may have one of the less healthy cereals and a scrambled egg. For a different approach to the lunch box sandwich, try these ideas:

Use two different kinds of bread; white on one side and wheat on the other. Out of bread? Use a hot dog or hamburger bun. It's bread, isn't it?

When a holiday comes around (Valentine's day, Halloween, St. Pat's, etc.), get out that food coloring! Put the food coloring in a shallow dish. With a paint brush, paint the edge of an appropriate cookie cutter and gently stamp a slice of bread for the sandwich.

For holiday sandwiches, bake bread or rolls in a mini-shaped or petite pan. There are several holiday pans offered on the market. Slice lengthwise and make the sandwiches.

Serve low-fat dressings, mayo, and sour cream in chilled pottery crocks and garnish with snipped chives or a sprig of dill or rosemary. Makes them feel more special.

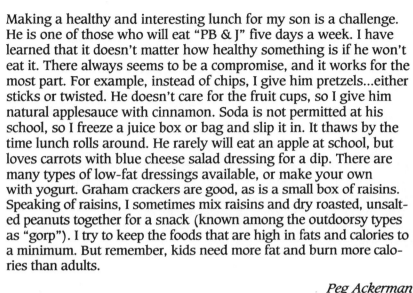

Making a healthy and interesting lunch for my son is a challenge. He is one of those who will eat "PB & J" five days a week. I have learned that it doesn't matter how healthy something is if he won't eat it. There always seems to be a compromise, and it works for the most part. For example, instead of chips, I give him pretzels...either sticks or twisted. He doesn't care for the fruit cups, so I give him natural applesauce with cinnamon. Soda is not permitted at his school, so I freeze a juice box or bag and slip it in. It thaws by the time lunch rolls around. He rarely will eat an apple at school, but loves carrots with blue cheese salad dressing for a dip. There are many types of low-fat dressings available, or make your own with yogurt. Graham crackers are good, as is a small box of raisins. Speaking of raisins, I sometimes mix raisins and dry roasted, unsalted peanuts together for a snack (known among the outdoorsy types as "gorp"). I try to keep the foods that are high in fats and calories to a minimum. But remember, kids need more fat and burn more calories than adults.

Peg Ackerman
Pasadena, CA

A good thing to remember when you have little ones is to get them to eat healthy foods and exercise every day. If they start when they're young, they will continue when they're adults. But remember that an occasional cookie always brings big smiles!

Crystal Parker
Gooseberry Patch Group Leader

A great, fun and healthy snack for children is made by slicing apples and bananas and serving them on a platter with toothpicks. Children spear the slices and dip them in a small bowl of dry strawberry or cherry gelatin.

Rebecca Suiter
Checotah, OK

81

To keep pasta sauce (alfredo or tomato) on hand in small amounts for my son, I freeze it in ice cube trays. Once frozen, I transfer it into a freezer bag. Two cubes is the perfect amount for 1 cup (dry) of pasta, and I don't have an open jar going bad in the fridge. This idea also works for leftover sauce.

Laurie Micarelli

My children love peanut butter sandwiches. I have found that the following ingredients combine well with peanut butter and are a great change from the standard peanut butter and jelly sandwich: honey, grated carrots, applesauce, cream cheese, toasted wheat germ, sliced bananas, raisins, bacon bits and cut-up dates.

Mary Bellizzi
Farmingville, NY

When my children were very small (and even now that they are older...they are 5 and 8) I make soups more enticing by adding pasta shaped like the A-B-Cs. The kids get so excited about spelling their names and recognizing letters, that they eat their way through healthy helpings of vegetable soup before they even realize it!

My neighbor suggested something that takes the pressure off one of the more difficult times for parents...dinner time. She keeps fresh veggies on hand chopped into bite-sized pieces. When the exhaustion, hunger and crankiness of the little ones kick in, a plateful of "appetizers" takes the edge off. We serve this to our kids with some light creamy Italian dressing as a dip, and they are in heaven!

Joanne Martin-Robinson

When my children come in from play asking for a snack, I have a rule we follow. First, they need to drink a cup of water. If this has not filled them up (it usually does), then they can have a healthy snack.

Lisa Sett
Thousand Oaks, CA

Vanilla or plain yogurt mixed with fruit is a refreshing combination, and if you are looking to find an on-the-go yummy-tummy filler, try blending yogurt with fruit, and/or fruit juice or skim milk to make a light drink full of protein and vitamin C. This is a great solution for young athletes on their way to practice during a busy schedule. It tastes good, is fairly light, and they can drink it on the go while still giving their body something substantial to eat.

Elizabeth H. Loffredo

Keep an ice cube tray or egg carton handy in the refrigerator with cut-up veggies, cheese, leftovers, etc. for grazing toddlers. They love the small portions and the independence of being able to get it themselves.

Mel Wolk
St. Peters, MO

A quick, easy snack my sister and I make are peeled sliced apples sprinkled with cinnamon sugar. It's like cold apple pie!

Heidi & Becky Walsh
Hingham, MA

Munchies & More

Homemade Bubbles

Renee, Emily, and Justin Hobler
Delaware, OH

My kids and I enjoy blowing bubbles. It's fun to see the different sizes and how far they will go before they pop! Sometimes we make our own:

1/3 c. thick dish soap
1 1/4 c. water
2 t. sugar

Combine ingredients and pour into an aluminum pie pan. Take a metal coat hanger and have an adult use pliers to bend the hanger into a straightened wire with a loop at the end. Use this to dip into the bubbles, and slowly wave it around!

Fun Dough

Mel Wolk
St. Peters, MO

2 c. white flour	**1 c. salt**
1 t. vanilla	**2 c. hot water**
4 t. cream of tartar	**2 T. salad oil**
	Food coloring

Mix dry ingredients. Add oil, water, and vanilla and cook over a low heat, stirring constantly until it forms a ball. Cool slightly and knead until smooth. Add food coloring and knead to blend. Store in a plastic bag or covered container. No refrigeration needed. Makes a huge ball of dough, or you can make three different colored balls (about 1 cup each). If you make your dough all one color, it is sometimes easier to color the water first, but it's not nearly as much fun as kneading the color into the warm lump.

Picnic Tablecloth

Wendy Lee Paffenroth
Pine Island, NY

Let your youngsters create a picnic tablecloth. Buy an inexpensive solid twin sheet, (a pastel color works well), some stencil paint and a few apples. Take the sheet and place on a hard surface (with protection underneath if this surface happens to be your kitchen table). Put a light coat of stencil paint on an old margarine lid. Cut the apples in half and dip into the paint, then press on the sheet along the border or use any design the children like. Different apples make different prints, so don't buy all the same variety or same size apples. Allow paint to dry. This can also be done with your children's handprints. It makes a great tablecloth, or let the kids throw it on the ground for a picnic. Years later, you will still be enjoying it!

Yummy Fruit Kabobs

Joan Rickert
North Pole, AK

These are a great, healthy treat for kids (and adults!) and fun to make and eat.

To make fruit kabobs, just cut into medium-sized chunks watermelon, cantaloupe and honeydew melons. Add strawberries, apples, bananas, cherries, grapes, or any fruit you like. Skewer the fruit onto wooden kabob sticks (available at most stores). We've used them as snacks for school parties, cookouts and picnics. Kids love the way these look and the fun of eating all the fruit off! Put a kabob in a glass of punch for a festive idea. (Please use your parental judgment when letting kids use the skewers.)

Say, "I love you."

Apple Kabobs

Peg Ackerman
Pasadena, CA

For a healthy snack in the lunch box, try these apple kabobs! Good and healthy, too!

1 apple, washed, unpeeled*,
   core removed, and cut in cubes
1/4 c. fresh lemon juice

1 c. Monterey Jack
   cheese (or Swiss or
   cheddar), cubed

Put lemon juice in small bowl. Dip the chunks of apples in the juice. (This keeps the apples from turning brown, and makes the apple taste great!) On wooden skewers, alternate cheese cubes and apple pieces. Wrap in plastic wrap and chill in refrigerator. Pack in lunch box. (Caution: skewers are for responsible older kids only!)

*I prefer to leave the peel on my apples...it just tastes better!

Mini Meatloaf Pies

Renee Hobler

1 lb. ground turkey,
   minced
1 t. Worcestershire sauce
1/2 c. bread crumbs
salt and pepper to taste

1 egg
2 T. dried onion
2 c. potato flakes,
   prepared
1/2 c. cheddar cheese,
   grated

Step 1: Wash your hands.

Step 2: Put all the ingredients except potato flakes and cheese in a bowl and mix with your hands. When it's all mixed up, spray medium size muffin tins with non-stick spray and fill each cup 3/4 full of meat mixture. Have an adult put them in the oven at 450 degrees for 15 minutes. While meatcups are baking, prepare the potato flakes using the directions on the package. When meat is done, spoon potatoes on top of meat and sprinkle with cheese. Put back in the oven until cheese melts. Serve with a side of green beans or your favorite green veggie!

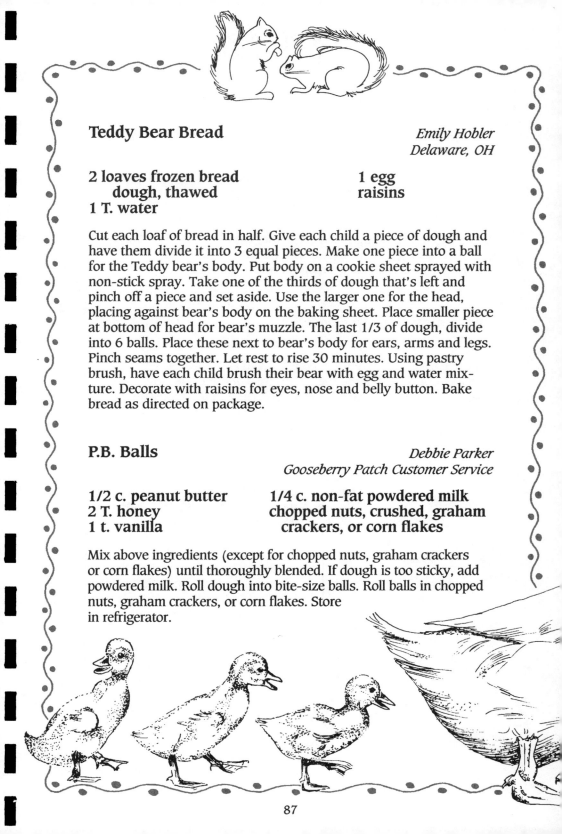

Teddy Bear Bread

Emily Hobler
Delaware, OH

2 loaves frozen bread
    dough, thawed
1 T. water

1 egg
raisins

Cut each loaf of bread in half. Give each child a piece of dough and have them divide it into 3 equal pieces. Make one piece into a ball for the Teddy bear's body. Put body on a cookie sheet sprayed with non-stick spray. Take one of the thirds of dough that's left and pinch off a piece and set aside. Use the larger one for the head, placing against bear's body on the baking sheet. Place smaller piece at bottom of head for bear's muzzle. The last 1/3 of dough, divide into 6 balls. Place these next to bear's body for ears, arms and legs. Pinch seams together. Let rest to rise 30 minutes. Using pastry brush, have each child brush their bear with egg and water mixture. Decorate with raisins for eyes, nose and belly button. Bake bread as directed on package.

P.B. Balls

Debbie Parker
Gooseberry Patch Customer Service

1/2 c. peanut butter
2 T. honey
1 t. vanilla

1/4 c. non-fat powdered milk
chopped nuts, crushed, graham
    crackers, or corn flakes

Mix above ingredients (except for chopped nuts, graham crackers or corn flakes) until thoroughly blended. If dough is too sticky, add powdered milk. Roll dough into bite-size balls. Roll balls in chopped nuts, graham crackers, or corn flakes. Store in refrigerator.

Munchies & More

Apple Smiles

Kimberly Burns

Enjoy your "smile."

1 red apple   **mini marshmallows**
peanut butter

Wash apple. Do not peel. Cut apple into eighths. Take two wedges for "lips" and spread peanut butter between. Place 4 to 5 marshmallows between "lips" for teeth. Makes 4 smiles.

Old-Timey Pop-up Popsicles

Louise Montillio

Where I grew up, there were no packaged popsicles, so we used to make our own. I make them with my children now, and their friends are always amazed that such scrumptious treats can be made by kids. They like them better than the store-bought kinds!

1 pkg. fruit-flavored drink mix   **just under 1 quart**
approximately 1 1/8 c. sugar   **water**

Using less than the suggested amount of water and more than the suggested amount of sugar, make up a strong batch of kid punch. Have the kids pour the liquid into paper cups and freeze. When ready, warm the cup slightly with your hands and pop the ice over, so the softer end is up. Give each child a spoon and tell them to dig away! They'll have to work a little harder, but they enjoy the task.

Butterfly Fruit Salad

Cheryl N. Berry
Gainesville, FL

When I was little, my mom would make me a special fruit salad that she learned to prepare in her days at nursing school. Little ones today love the idea of eating a salad that is a "picture."

2 maraschino cherries, with stems
1/2 c. low-fat cottage cheese
2 canned peach halves
lettuce leaf
1 canned pear half

Place lettuce leaf on plate. Place pear half with hole facing up. Place scoop of cottage cheese into hole of pear half. Place peach halves cut-side down on either side of the pear half. Place stems of cherries against the top narrow part of the pear half so they resemble antennae. Now let your little ones enjoy eating their very own butterfly!

Party Lemonade

Gizelle Robinson
Hingham, MA

Try this recipe for your child's next birthday party. It's sure to make them feel special!

maraschino cherries
12 oz. pink frozen lemonade, thawed
1 liter sugar-free carbonated lemon-lime drink
straws

Put cherries in each section of an ice cube tray, fill with water, and freeze. Mix lemonade as directed. Add lemon-lime drink and ice cubes. Enjoy!

Everyone should own a rocking chair...
such a simple pleasure!

Pudding Bars

Debbie Parker
Gooseberry Patch Customer Service

1 1/2 c. cold milk
1/2 c. creamy peanut butter
4 oz. pkg. instant pudding

20 whole graham crackers

In a medium bowl, put milk, peanut butter, and pudding. Beat mixture, at low speed, until well blended. Let stand for five minutes until mixture is thick. Break graham crackers in half. Spread pudding mixture about half inch thick on twenty graham cracker halves. Top with other half of graham cracker. Wrap each individual bar in plastic wrap or aluminum foil. Freeze until firm (about 3 to 4 hours).

Finger Juice (Healthy Finger Gelatin)

Mel Wolk
St. Peters, MO

1 c. water
3 T. unflavored gelatin

6 oz. juice concentrate (thawed)

Put water in saucepan and sprinkle gelatin on top. When it softens, heat until dissolved (or microwave for 30 seconds). Add juice and blend well. Pour into a flat 8" square pan and chill until set. Cut into 1" squares or use Gooseberry cookie cutters to cut out shapes. Serve as a finger food; it stays firm at room temperature. Two cups of fresh or bottled juice can be substituted for the water and concentrate. For Easter, you can pour the juice mixture into eggshells or deviled egg molds.

Eggs in a Nest

Mel Wolk
St. Peters, MO

2 slices of whole wheat bread   2 eggs
pat of butter

Butter a slice of whole wheat bread. Cut a hole in the center of the bread with a biscuit or cookie cutter, and remove center. Toast bread in a hot skillet. Gently crack an egg inside the hole while toasting. Carefully turn and cook until desired doneness. You may wish to cover after turning. Place egg and toast onto a plate. Grill the bread cut-out and use it to hide the egg (great for dipping). Small children love the surprise.

Snack Attack

Renee Hobler
Gooseberry Patch Customer Service

1/2 c. dried apricots, banana chips,   1/2 c. candy-coated
**   other dried fruit, chopped   pieces**
3 c. granola   1/2 c. peanuts
1/2 c. dates, chopped or diced   1/2 c. raisins

Stir everything together in a large bowl. Cover and store unrefrigerated.

Cow Shake

Tucker Robinson
Hingham, MA

3/4 c. milk
2 tsp. cocoa
2 t. honey
1 ice cube

Mix in blender for
a terrific treat!

Mini Fruit Pizzas

Becky Malone

Toppings:

Fresh Fruit (cut into pieces): Strawberries, grapes, melon, kiwi, pineapple, bananas, blueberries, etc.

Frosting: (0 grams of fat)

13-oz. jar of marshmallow cream
2 8-oz. pkgs. of fat-free cream cheese

Crust:

1 pkg. refrigerated sugar cookie dough

Bake sugar cookies according to directions on package. Allow to cool. Mix cream cheese and marshmallow cream with electric mixer. Frost cookies with mixture and top with fresh fruit. This is a creative way for kids to enjoy fresh fruit and use their imagination.

Baby's Health Crackers

Mel Wolk
St. Peters, MO

2 1/2 c. whole wheat flour, sifted	3 T. oil
2 t. wheat germ	3 T. honey
2 T. soy flour	2/3 c. milk
2 T. non-fat dry milk powder	1 t. vanilla

Mix together the dry ingredients. Combine the oil, honey, milk and vanilla. Blend the liquid ingredients into the dry ingredients and knead until they form a smooth ball. If the dough is too dry, add water or milk one drop at a time without letting it get too soft. Roll out on a floured surface about 1/4" thick and cut into shapes with floured cookie cutter. Bake at 350 degrees on greased baking sheet for 10 to 12 minutes. Don't let it get too brown. Remove and cool on wire racks. Store in tightly covered container. This will make about a dozen large teething crackers.

Cookie Cutter Sandwiches

Tonny Guido
Harrison, NY

A special treat for the children...my nieces and nephews love to come to lunch, especially when I make "cookie cutter sandwiches."

a favorite cookie cutter of the child's choice
2 slices of bread
whatever filling the child prefers

If the child is old enough, he or she can help make the sandwich... peanut butter and jelly, grilled cheese, cold cuts, tuna or egg salad... any favorite sandwich filling will do. After you prepare the sandwich, the kids love to use the cookie cutter themselves on it. For some reason this makes it taste "oh so much better!" On the holidays you can use trees, stars and Santas for Christmas, hearts for Valentine's Day and bunnies for Easter, etc.

"I Love You" Pancakes

Mel Wolk
St. Peters, MO

Using a small spoon, drizzle pancake batter onto a griddle in the shape of a little heart. After a few seconds, pour a regular-sized pancake shape on top of the heart. When you turn it over, the heart will show up a little darker. You can make designs, faces, numbers, or even write messages or names (write backwards so it comes out right-reading). If you're doing a lot of these, you may wish to use a squeeze bottle like an empty honey bear.

Sugar Sandwiches for Kids

Jeannine English
Wylie, TX

I've always used these sandwiches as a special treat for heartbroken or sick kids, or whenever a special treat is called for. Simple, but you'll be famous with the kids! My kids used to call them "Mom's famous sandwiches."

2 slices bread
butter or margarine
sugar to taste

bit of honey
cinnamon

Use whatever bread you have on hand and spread with butter or margarine. Sprinkle a little granulated sugar or squeeze a bit of honey onto the butter. You can also add a sprinkle of cinnamon. Put another piece of bread on top and then cut shapes with cookie cutters.

Teddy Bear's Picnic Cupcakes

Joanne Martin-Robinson

This is a great idea for in-school birthday parties or equally important occasions when you want to do something special for your child, but you (of course) don't have a lot of time!

cake mix
white frosting mix
cocktail umbrellas

Teddy bear-shaped
graham crackers

Make cake mix according to directions. Pour into paper liners in a cupcake tin as you would when making any cupcake or muffin. Bake the cupcakes as directed. Make the frosting according to directions, being sure to add green food coloring to create the "grass" for the Teddy bear's picnic. Frost each cupcake completely with green frosting. "Sit" a couple of Teddy bears on top of each cupcake, then open an umbrella and stick on top of the cupcake to shade the bears. The kids just love them, and they're easier to make than they look...my kind of recipe!

Instant Banana Pudding

Mel Wolk
St. Peters, MO

2 bananas, ripe   2 T. peanut butter
1/2 c. applesauce   2 T. honey

Mix until smooth and chill. Makes about 4 servings.

Banana Bug Breakfast

Joyce Howardson
Morganville, NJ

No cooking is required for this recipe; even your child can make this. My son, now 13, loved this breakfast when he was younger, because he could make it himself (except for slicing the banana). Once in a while he still has one for breakfast. This is great for picky eaters!

1 banana, ripe
2 T. peanut butter (you can use low-fat, if you wish)
6 or 7 raisins, more if you like

Slice banana into slices. "Glue" the slices back together again with the peanut butter. Again using the peanut butter, "glue" the raisins on the banana making a face on one end of the banana and decorating the body with whatever is left.

Munchies & More

Fresh Applesauce

Margaret Towne
San Jose, CA

This is a fun recipe to make with children. The frozen banana makes the applesauce icy cold.

1 frozen banana
3 large green apples
1/4 t. cinnamon

1/4 t. nutmeg
1/2 c. apple juice

Peel, slice, wrap (in plastic) and freeze the banana. Peel the apples, set one aside, core and chop the other two. Put the frozen banana, the two chopped apples, cinnamon, nutmeg and apple juice into blender or food processor. Blend until smooth. Pour into a bowl and grate in the other apple. Stir and serve. Serves 4.

ABC Soup with Cheese and Crackers

Emily Hobler
Delaware, OH

6 c. chicken broth
1/2 c. celery, chopped
1/4 c. onion, diced
2 c. frozen mixed veggies

6 oz. uncooked alphabet
    macaroni
2 c. chicken, cooked,
    chunked

Heat broth and veggies to a boil. Add macaroni and reduce heat. Cook 15 minutes or until ABCs are tender. Stir in chicken and simmer until chicken is hot. Serve with side crackers and cheese. Just melt the cheese on top for a few seconds in the microwave.

Ants on a Log

Rebecca Suiter
Checotah, OK

Children love to make this healthy and fun treat!

celery stick
raisins

peanut butter

Stuff a celery stick with peanut butter and line the little ants (raisins) up in a row on the peanut butter.

Fruit Juice Pops

Debbie Parker
Gooseberry Patch Customer Service

6 oz. can frozen juice concentrate
1 to 2 T. sugar or honey

16 ozs. plain yogurt
1 t. vanilla

Blend ingredients in a blender. Pour into small cups or popsicle molds. Insert sticks when mixture is partially frozen. Freeze until firm.

Frozen fruit pops are frosty and refreshing! Just slice up your favorite fruits like kiwi, strawberries, grapes, peaches, oranges and bananas and freeze them in their own natural juices.

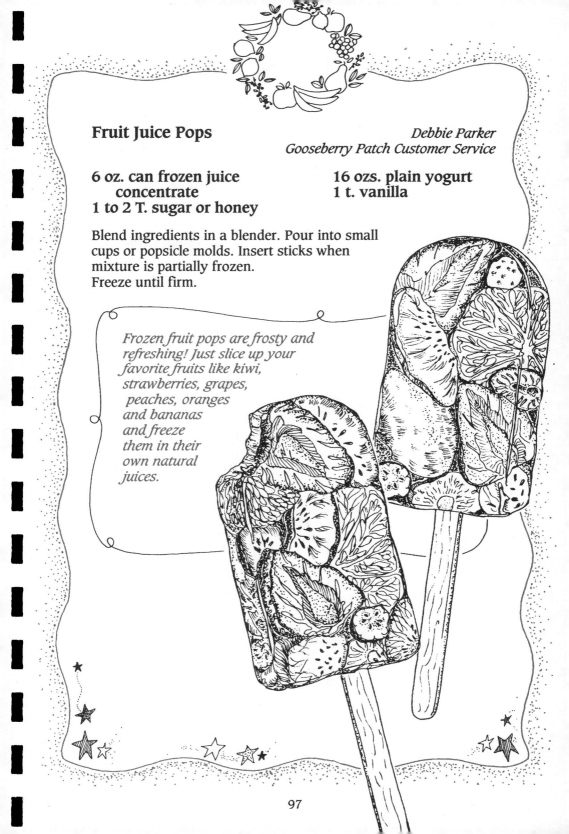

Munchies & More

Bumpy Peanut Butter Balls

Tammy Barnum
Portland, TN

Your kids will love these healthy snacks, and so will you!

1/2 c. natural peanut butter
1/4 c. non-fat dry milk powder
1/4 c. unsweetened coconut, shredded
1/4 c. apple juice concentrate, thawed

1/3 c. rolled oats
1/2 t. cinnamon
1/4 c. wheat germ
1/4 c. raisins, chopped

Combine all ingredients in a large mixing bowl and mix thoroughly. Shape into 1" balls. Place on a cookie sheet and chill thoroughly before serving. Store in refrigerator. Makes 30 small balls.

Bagel Snack

Emily and Justin Hobler
Delaware, OH

1/2 c. peanut butter
2 T. honey

3 bagels or English muffins
dried fruit bits, fresh fruit or shelled sunflower seeds

Measure peanut butter and honey and stir together in a small bowl. Toast bagel halves or English muffins in toaster. Cut bagel or muffin halves into 4 pieces with scissors or knife with an adult's help. Spread with peanut butter mixture and sprinkle with bits of dried fruit, sunflower seeds or sliced bananas. Don't wait! Serve right away.

Breakfast Burritos

Peg Ackerman
Pasadena, CA

For a quick breakfast on Saturday morning, before the little league game or "shop-a-thon" at the mall, we sometimes have breakfast burritos! Great for a breakfast on the run!

tortillas (we use flour)
grated cheese of your choice
scrambled eggs
hot sauce or salsa (totally optional...it's a husband thing!)

Warm the tortillas in the microwave. Put some grated cheese on the tortilla, then the scrambled egg and salsa (if you want). Wrap like a burrito, serve with orange juice and a piece of fruit! You can add bacon, sausage or Canadian bacon, too!

Cream Cheese "Pie"

Lynda Tatman
Fresno, CA

This came quite by accident one night. We all had a sweet tooth and wanted something quick and easy. It has been a favorite, even to us grown ups. Everyone thinks this tastes like a cream cheese pie.

graham crackers   **fresh strawberries**
low-fat cream cheese

Take the graham crackers and spread them with low-fat cream cheese. Wash and stem strawberries. Put in a small bowl and chill. Use a dinner plate and put the small bowl of strawberries in the middle. Place the graham cracker squares with cream cheese around the small bowl on the plate.

Peanut Butter Play Clay

Mel Wolk
St. Peters, MO

1/2 c. peanut butter   **a bit of honey**
3 1/2 T. powdered milk
   (non-instant works best)

Mix together above ingredients, roll into balls and store in refrigerator. Kids love to play with this, and then eat their creations! For fancy candy, let them add coconut, wheat germ, nuts, seeds, or raisins and roll into small balls. Chill. Makes about 1/2 cup of play clay.

*Give little
unexpected gifts...
it will make
you feel good!*

100

Food for the Soul

Heartwarming stories that make you feel good

Make your own "special moments." Last Christmas, a person very dear to our family was experiencing some tragic health problems. After a very stressful week, I arrived home from work to find that UPS had delivered a package from my two nieces. I hurried into the house, dragging the package, set down my purse and without much thought started to open the box. The first thing that caught my eye was some beautiful red cellophane; then a tiny golden angel fluttered down as I pulled apart the top layer. I knew this was to be a "special moment." I immediately stopped unwrapping and took time to prepare. I put on the tea kettle, warmed my tea cup, set a log in the fire, turned on some soft Christmas music, waited for my tea, and gave myself a moment to calm down. After settling in by the fire with my freshly brewed tea, I began to open the package. More tiny angels fluttered all around. The sweet smell of apples and cinnamon filled the air. I found inside the box three wonderfully wrapped gifts from my nieces and great-niece. I took the time, right there, before Christmas to make this a moment to enjoy these beautiful gifts from the heart from three girls who care about me. I savored each gift, and read in peace and solitude the beautiful words written to me. I could think about each sentence, I could envision when they were written, the sincerity and love put into each thought. I felt so very loved. This "special moment" comes back to me every time I look at the lovely gifts they sent. Make those special moments count, learn to recognize when they appear, prepare for them. Take the time, you'll never regret it.

Pat Akers
Stanton, CA

Our baby-sitter took my five-year-old son for a walk the other day. As they walked by the cemetery on the main street near our home, my son observed the display of gravestones with innocent wonder and inquired, "Don't you think it's silly that everyone dies under stones?" A child's perspective is truly a wonderful thing!

Joanne Martin-Robinson

Living out in the country and being home-bound quite a bit, the wildlife here has become a calming, charming, and interesting part of my life. I feed the birds, squirrels, and rabbits, and feel that we commune with one another. Daily cares seem forgotten when staring one-to-one with a squirrel through the window! The squirrels especially seem to each have a unique personality; therefore, naming them makes perfect sense to me. I can always tell which squirrel is which. For instance, the main one that stares at me through the window is "Nutty" because he gets a little frown on his face, complete with wrinkled brow. When fresh sunflower seeds aren't in the tray, he jumps onto my window screen and hangs there until he gets what he wants. Another squirrel nicknamed "Swifty" does gymnastics by himself in the yard. No matter how much physical pain I'm in that day (from arthritis,) they make me forget and focus on more positive thoughts. As I say, they are my friends, and I believe the world moves too fast a pace these days. Stopping to appreciate and commune with nature brings us back to a fuller, richer existence, calming jangled nerves. It's hard to feel really negative when you really listen to a sweet little wren's song, or feed some dried corn to the old duck named "Charlie" who comes visiting each day.

Barbara Loe
Burleson, TX

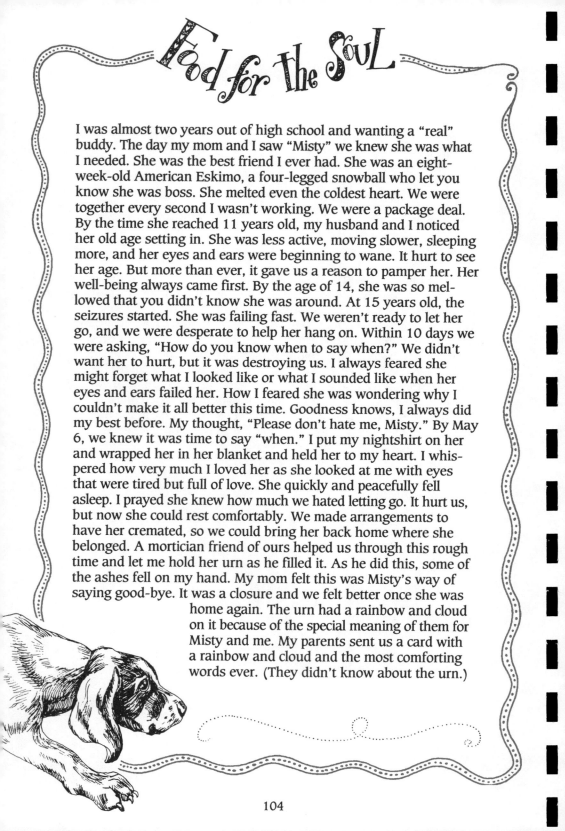

Food for the Soul

I was almost two years out of high school and wanting a "real" buddy. The day my mom and I saw "Misty" we knew she was what I needed. She was the best friend I ever had. She was an eight-week-old American Eskimo, a four-legged snowball who let you know she was boss. She melted even the coldest heart. We were together every second I wasn't working. We were a package deal. By the time she reached 11 years old, my husband and I noticed her old age setting in. She was less active, moving slower, sleeping more, and her eyes and ears were beginning to wane. It hurt to see her age. But more than ever, it gave us a reason to pamper her. Her well-being always came first. By the age of 14, she was so mellowed that you didn't know she was around. At 15 years old, the seizures started. She was failing fast. We weren't ready to let her go, and we were desperate to help her hang on. Within 10 days we were asking, "How do you know when to say when?" We didn't want her to hurt, but it was destroying us. I always feared she might forget what I looked like or what I sounded like when her eyes and ears failed her. How I feared she was wondering why I couldn't make it all better this time. Goodness knows, I always did my best before. My thought, "Please don't hate me, Misty." By May 6, we knew it was time to say "when." I put my nightshirt on her and wrapped her in her blanket and held her to my heart. I whispered how very much I loved her as she looked at me with eyes that were tired but full of love. She quickly and peacefully fell asleep. I prayed she knew how much we hated letting go. It hurt us, but now she could rest comfortably. We made arrangements to have her cremated, so we could bring her back home where she belonged. A mortician friend of ours helped us through this rough time and let me hold her urn as he filled it. As he did this, some of the ashes fell on my hand. My mom felt this was Misty's way of saying good-bye. It was a closure and we felt better once she was home again. The urn had a rainbow and cloud on it because of the special meaning of them for Misty and me. My parents sent us a card with a rainbow and cloud and the most comforting words ever. (They didn't know about the urn.)

It did wonders for us. The day after she passed we found a mini rose bush named "Rainbow's End." We knew we would be all right. In the couple weeks that followed, we missed out on two female Sheltie pups and it upset my husband. I told him there was a reason; God has a plan. The end of May, we met our Godsend, a Sheltie breeder to top them all. In June a litter of three pups ended up being only one, a female. She was promised to another couple and they never inquired about her. The breeder said she was ours. As a result, she is named "Misty's Special Delivery." We feel Misty made sure this puppy was for us. We call her Molly Sue and love her dearly, although Misty is forever in our hearts and minds. Since we picked her up, she has worn the bell from Misty's harness. The bell didn't phase me until I heard it in the house again for the first time since Misty passed. The effect it had on my heart and spirits was indescribable. A part of us left with Misty, and Molly is helping to make each day easier. But we'll never forget the best buddy we ever had.

Robin Reese
Fremont, OH

Hug your kids or dog or someone every day!

My grandmother used to sew for everyone in our family; she made dresses for my two sisters and me when we were little. She saved every extra button, piece of lace and scrap of fabric. The smaller scraps were put in my doll clothes box for creating new fashions. With the larger pieces she made patchwork quilts, and she gave me one when my daughter was born. It was really special to have a quilt for my daughter that came from my childhood. And, as for the buttons (antiques now), when Grandma died she left them to me—probably because I used to spend hours going though her button box! I use the really unusual ones; the ones of bone, mother-of-pearl, or ceramic...the colorful cut-out plastic ones...the ones with marcasites and rhinestones...to dress up a vest, shirt or dress. And, recently I recovered some pillows and embellished them with a few of the especially big, ornate buttons. Every time I look at them I think of Grandma, the creative gifts she had, and how she shared them.

When my children were small and money was tight, we lived in one half of a double; my landlady lived in the other half. Sometimes on cold winter days when we'd get home from work and school, I'd find a big pot of vegetable soup from Mrs. Cramer steaming on the front porch. The soup was delicious, filled with carrots, potatoes, corn, lima beans, cabbage, tomatoes and onion in a flavorful broth. A pleasant departure from our usual macaroni and cheese or beans and weenies, it was a wonderful treat to sit down with my kids and enjoy this gift. At other times, Mrs.Cramer would slip a jar of homemade jam and some fresh bread inside my front door. These kindnesses from Mrs. Cramer did more than satisfy our appetites; they lifted our spirits and taught my children the value of giving. My kids and I enjoyed returning the favor with homemade cards, cookies and special errands. Sometimes, the smallest gestures..."random acts of kindness"...can make the biggest difference in people's lives.

Molly Bordonaro

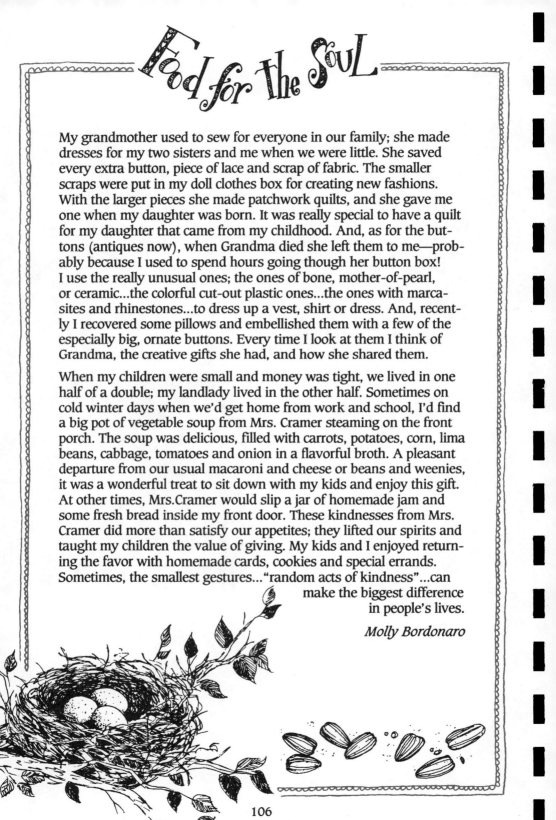

When I was ten years old, a new family began to attend my church. Mr. and Mrs. Clark had six children. I was from a broken home and was instantly drawn to them. They were a happy, stable, loving family, and I longed to become a part of their family unit. The Clark family often took me home with them on Sunday afternoons. It was in their home that I learned what unconditional love and acceptance were all about. Mr. and Mrs. Clark unselfishly gave their love and time to me, and taught me discipline, perseverance, and responsibility. They eventually allowed me to call them "Mama" and "Papa," and their children accepted me as a sibling. I could never begin to express my gratitude for the influence they have had in my life. All that I am today, I owe to them and their willingness to reach out to a lonely little girl. They have been instrumental in building my self-esteem and teaching me the values of faith in God that have stayed with me until this day. I am able to reach out and embrace others because they were willing to reach out and embrace me.

Charlotte M. Rissler
Manheim, PA

After an awfully windy rainstorm, I noticed a mother robin tending to her three fluffy chicks on the ground...blown out of an oak tree, nest and all. I gently picked up the nest and chicks, and placed them into a large empty plastic hanging pot, then hung the pot on a protected branch. I watched in amazement as the mother bird continued to feed her brood in their "new home"! It was funny to watch the flowerpot sway gently in the breeze, all the time knowing the chicks were safe inside. As the chicks grew, all three would perch on the edge of the flowerpot to be fed. It was then I knew they were going to make it! I realized how powerful we humans can be. Sometimes, with the simplest gestures, we can save the lives of nature's most fragile creatures.

Jan Walsh
Gooseberry Patch Illustrator

Food for the Soul

One of my most treasured gifts is a yellow quilt with a basket design, and it hangs in my living room from the quilt rack my husband made. I would like to share with you what I see when I look at my quilt.

I see my neighbor lady with tears in her eyes and hands extended out to me with the yellow quilt resting on them and saying, "Here I want you to have this." You see, my neighbor lady was moving from her big house to a smaller one due to failing health.

I see my neighbor early in the morning with her ladder resting against her cherry tree and her on it picking cherries.

I see her at my door with fresh baked pies, cookies, and sweet rolls; the day I started my diet.

I see her at my door with an angel food cake for a special event like confirmation or graduation.

I see her going from house to house in the neighborhood with plates of goodies.

I see my son sitting beside her, outside the church on a cold winter's day, where she lay on the ice after falling.

I see her asking for my husband when she lay dying. She was partial to my husband and the boys, and we often wondered if that was because she lost her only son in the war.

I see her lying peacefully in the church she loved, surrounded by friends and family saying goodbye. I see the gift every day, the gift of caring, sharing and loving.

Sue Duncan
Sac City, IA

Two years ago in December, I got married and my future mother-in-law made my wedding dress. It was gorgeous and took months to make. Sometimes my mother-in-law would work on pieces of the dress at the nursing home where her 94-year-old mother lived. As the wedding date neared closer, the day came for my bridal portrait to be taken. We decided to stop by the nursing home first. We weren't sure if her mother would be able to make it to the wedding, and wanted to give her a special preview. We arrived at the nursing home and I put the dress on and stepped out in the hallway so she could see the dress. A few nurses came down the hall to admire it, as well. My mother-in-law went to the car to get her camera, and while she was gone her mother started to cry...then the nurses began to cry. The nurses suggested that I walk down to the living room so everyone could see my dress. Even though I was embarrassed and refused, they talked me into it. As I walked into the room, (with the nurses, my mother-in-law, and grandmother following) an elderly lady who had been playing folk songs on the piano began to play "Here Comes the Bride." Everyone in the room stopped what they were doing to ooh and ahh. It amazed me though to see all the gloomy faces light up with excitement. The next week my husband and I were married and his grandmother did attend the ceremony. That was two years ago, and this year at the age of 96, our grandmother passed away. I was embarrassed at the time, but now this is one of the most special memories of our wedding that I know I will cherish forever.

Penny Ticknor
Sherman, TX

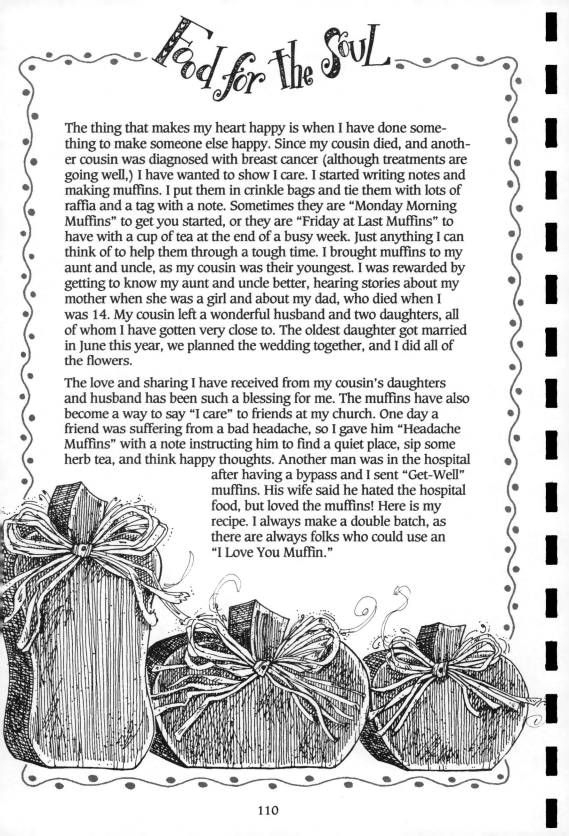

Food for the Soul

The thing that makes my heart happy is when I have done something to make someone else happy. Since my cousin died, and another cousin was diagnosed with breast cancer (although treatments are going well,) I have wanted to show I care. I started writing notes and making muffins. I put them in crinkle bags and tie them with lots of raffia and a tag with a note. Sometimes they are "Monday Morning Muffins" to get you started, or they are "Friday at Last Muffins" to have with a cup of tea at the end of a busy week. Just anything I can think of to help them through a tough time. I brought muffins to my aunt and uncle, as my cousin was their youngest. I was rewarded by getting to know my aunt and uncle better, hearing stories about my mother when she was a girl and about my dad, who died when I was 14. My cousin left a wonderful husband and two daughters, all of whom I have gotten very close to. The oldest daughter got married in June this year, we planned the wedding together, and I did all of the flowers.

The love and sharing I have received from my cousin's daughters and husband has been such a blessing for me. The muffins have also become a way to say "I care" to friends at my church. One day a friend was suffering from a bad headache, so I gave him "Headache Muffins" with a note instructing him to find a quiet place, sip some herb tea, and think happy thoughts. Another man was in the hospital after having a bypass and I sent "Get-Well" muffins. His wife said he hated the hospital food, but loved the muffins! Here is my recipe. I always make a double batch, as there are always folks who could use an "I Love You Muffin."

Pumpkin Muffins

I have tried to make these muffins more healthy by adding less sugar and less fat, but have decided to stick to the muffins I know will taste good!

1 1/2 c. sugar	1 t. allspice	1/4 c. vegetable oil
1/2 t. salt	1 3/4 c. flour	1 c. pumpkin
1 t. baking soda	2 eggs	1/4 c. milk
1 t. cinnamon		

Heat oven to 350 degrees. In a large bowl, sift together sugar, salt, baking soda, cinnamon, allspice, and flour. In another bowl, mix together eggs, oil, pumpkin, and milk. Add wet mixture to dry and mix lightly just to blend. Fill greased muffin tin half-way and bake for 25 to 30 minutes. Pumpkin pie spice can be substituted for cinnamon and allspice. Cool in pan for five minutes, then remove from pan. Makes 12 muffins.

I like to see children having a good time out in nature, so I have "Herb Picnics" for the first and second graders at a local Christian school. One year our theme was peppermint, so we made peppermint peanut butter sandwiches which we cut into heart and Teddy bear shapes. We had grape and peppermint punch, and we finished with peppermint chocolate chip cookies and peppermint ice cream. The picnic was set up near the herb gardens. After the children ate, we had a "touch, taste, and smell" time where we learned about the ways herbs were used in the olden days. The children loved the soft feel of the Lamb's Ear, and liked learning how it was used as a bandage by pioneer mothers when their children had a small cut. The smell of lemon, thyme, pineapple sage and others kept them asking questions. We dug up a peppermint plant and saw how it spreads underground by its roots, and that nothing can stop its spread unless you put something in its way. I shared how this is like the love we have in our hearts; we cannot stop it from spreading. We talked about how we can share our love, and then we potted a peppermint plant for each child to take home. They were all excited about planting their "love plant." It was so nice to see the yellow school bus full of happy faces, waving with one hand, and holding tightly to their "love plant" with the other!

Elizabeth Timmins

In mid-spring of this year, while I was cutting tulips, my son Chance was using the stems for a magic wand. He was waving his wand over my head asking what I wanted to be turned into. I thought for a moment, then replied "A beautiful woman." He stared at me, put one hand on his hip, rolled his eyes and innocently informed me, "I don't have that kind of magic, do you want to be a worm?"

On the way to preschool, there is a cemetery. One day, my four-year-old son asked me what that place was. I told him that after people die they are buried there. His follow-up question was, "Why are there flowers there?" I told him after people die, people who are alive bring flowers to the grave so the ones who have died know that they still miss and think about them. That answer seemed to satisfy him. He didn't say anything else until we were saying good-bye at his classroom door. He looked at me with his big brown eyes and said, "Mom, when you die, I'm gonna put flowers there so I can remember where I planted you!"

Tracey Monnetta
Roseville, MI

As a mother of ten children, I have many heartwarming stories. My twin girls were born the eighth and ninth in the family and were a complete surprise to everyone! Years ago that could happen! When I brought them home from the hospital, I put them together in one crib to keep them safe from the other seven kids (two of whom were inquisitive toddlers). I heard a peculiar noise coming from their room and went to investigate. There were my enterprising older sons with a ladder up to the window, charging everyone in the neighborhood 2¢ a peek.

When my son Peter was taking his first communion, his father and I and five siblings were there. As all of the children proceeded past us, the priest leaned over and told us it was time we get another bath-room. All through the service we were puzzled about what he said. Afterward, we questioned the priest. He told us that during Peter's confession he admitted that he didn't say his morning prayers. When asked why he said, "Father, if you lived in my house and had to stand in line for the bathroom, you'd forget your prayers, too!"

Jean Martin
Hingham, MA

Three years ago, I was diagnosed with breast cancer. Instead of being a death sentence, which is how I first perceived it, it has become a turning point in my life. During my course of surgery and treatment I met wonderful and understanding doctors, nurses and other patients. I began to see that having cancer is not the end but can be the beginning of a wonderful life to live, if only I can see it. I see the beauty in life now...the flowers and trees, the stars at night while the crickets sing, and my children's laughter. I am also able to be myself without worry of what others think and to do things for myself, instead of doing only for others. Inability to please everyone in the past led to a lot of frustration and resentment on my part. Today, I do things for others because I enjoy it. There are still chores and things that have to be done, but basically I am living for myself and not trying to please everyone else. I have become comfortable with who I am and am no longer afraid of making mistakes, because I realize that mistakes are all a part of being human and learning. I try to live my life one day at a time, because I don't know what the future might hold. But I am eager to find out the good as well as the bad. At 36, I have finally learned that I must take care of myself, which includes my body. To eat healthy and exercise which has improved my mental attitude and how well I feel. Today I am a cancer survivor, and grateful to God for every day that I have. Instead of living always for tomorrow, I live for today, and enjoy my life.

Linda Moore
Midland, TX

My mother loved to make Christmas candles. Red ones, white ones, round ones and square ones. She would group them in stair-step style on the mantle. The fat, squatty ones would be set on a bed of pine all by themselves. The living and dining rooms would be aglow with the soft, warm light, welcoming the most holy of holidays. I have just one candle left that my mother made. I light it just on Christmas Eve, in her honor.

Peg Ackerman
Pasadena, CA

I am the oldest of three girls in my family. When our mother died suddenly three years ago, we had the task of going through her clothing. All three of us had special memories of certain items she wore, but most especially her blue chenille robe. It represented our warm, loving mama. I took the robe home (secretly) and came up with an idea for each of us to have a "piece" of the robe. My mother collected Teddy bears, as bears were the mascot of the school where she worked. I had a co-worker sew three bears from the robe for Christmas gifts last year. I also had a Christmas plaid taffeta blouse I had given to Mama several years ago. My friend made the bears out of the robe and then made collars out of the blouse. I could hardly wait for Christmas morning to present my sisters and daughter with my extra special gift. Needless to say, my bears were the "tear-jerker" gifts! All three of us now look at our bears and remember how mama loved us all.

Phyllis Stout
East Palatka, FL

Sort out, clean closets, organize! Once a year, pretend that you're going to move and there's no way you can take it all with you.

114

During one's lifetime, we can receive many gifts. Some are meant to last, while others are given just for the moment. While I was in the process of growing up, I never considered my mother's gifts of any value, simply because I didn't know that I had been given any. (Mothers have a way of slipping these things under your nose.) These gifts that I'm speaking of consist of teaching a child the way things are and the way they should be. Mothers can show you how to get back on your feet when life throws you a curve. I'm sorry to say that, in today's world, some mothers have lost the ability to communicate with their own children. My sister and I were taught independence at an early age. We were given the gift of kindness and understanding, to both humans and animals. Patience was given on a daily basis, sprinkled with morals. The best gift that we have been given is the ability to laugh and not take this world too seriously. Humor played such a big part in our upbringing. When I think about it, I must have kept those precious gifts inside of me. Life has thrown us one final curve; my mother died not so long ago. Without her "gifts" to us, life would have been a lot tougher to bear. Thanks, Mom, for just being you!

Deborah Settle
Strongstown, PA

One of my warmest memories of my mother is a trip that she made to visit us in Germany. It occurred while we were on a bus trip to Holland. We had been traveling for a few days with the same group of people, and when we arrived at one of the stops along the way, Mom opted to remain on the bus and rest. As she had heart problems, she was tired. She thought everyone had emptied the bus when a young service man came up behind her and presented her with a lovely bouquet of tulips he had purchased at a flower stand. He said that she reminded him of someone that he missed and loved very much. Mom was very touched over this gesture, as were we. Five years later my mother passed away. I always feel so happy as I recall this day. What a warm special memory!

Delores Hollenbeck
Omaha, NE

Smile! It's contagious.

Food for The Soul

What is a Friend?

A friend is somebody who hears your woes,
Who's always beside you however life goes.
Who's glad when you're happy and blue when you're sad,
Who sees all your good points, overlooks all your bad.

A friend is somebody who gives you a lift,
According to some, a friend is a gift,
Not one that you buy or select from a shelf,

But a friend is a gift that you give yourself.
As I start each day and end each day too, I whisper,
"Thank heaven I met one like you!"

Reflection

The mirror flashed a picture of a woman old and gray.
I hardly recognized her
As the girl of yesterday
And yet, I did not feel that old
My heart was young and gay.
Remembering the years gone by
As just the other day.
How could this mirror on the wall
Reflect this old, old face
Sadly I remembered
This was still the same old place
That I had lived while in my youth
Much fairer in that day.
Grown older now,
That image seems very far away
Yet I still recall
Without any fear or shame,
The reflection may be different
But the heart is still the same.

Maxine Smith
Ogden, UT

Just recently, the mother of a dear friend of mine passed away at the young age of 59. She suffered with breast cancer just like other members of her family before her. Because she knew that she was predisposed to the disease, she did everything "correct," nursed five children, never smoked and never ate red meat. None of that seemed to matter, because this cancer caught up with her and took her very quickly. My friend and her family were all with their mother when she died. She was suffering terribly, but the family held strong and sang to her, spoke with her and gave her their permission to die. When my friend (who is 32 weeks pregnant) was speaking to her mother for one of the last times, she told her, as she passes away and crosses paths with her unborn child, to give the child a hug. How strong my friend had to be to say something like that to her mother! I have been deeply affected by her mother's death and the strength of my friend. She has always been one to look at her children and say, "What else in this world could be more important than the raising of these children and giving them decent morals and values?" As family-oriented as she is, her mother's death has seemed to put everything into perspective even more. She said that her mother entered into this world beautiful and she left it even more beautiful. The most important thing that happened in between those two events were the relationships that she built with those around her. You leave this world with nothing except those relationships, so put everything that you have into them and cherish them. I consider myself a very lucky person to have a friend like her, and I definitely cherish my friendship with her.

S. Parkinson
Lompoc, CA

I Love You, Dad

I find myself once again
Silently crying unexpectedly,
As the pain of my loss
Returns with a vengeance.
I miss you so much, Dad.
Our talks, the walks in the backyard,
The joy of seeing you with my son...
Your existence as a human being.

Oh, child of mine, don't weep for me.
For I see and hear and feel
Much more than you know.
I am the intricate crystals of snow
Flowing gently from the heavens,
I am the frost on your windowpanes,
The rain nourishing the earth,
The wind rustling the autumn leaves.
I am the early morning sunshine
Glistening through the branches of the trees.
I am the stars shining softly in the dark night sky,
And the harvest moon lighting your way.
I am the burst of color that spans the horizon
As the sun rises and sets.
My soul is free and soaring
with the eagles.
So dry your eyes.
And please,
don't stand at my grave
and cry.
I am not there,
I did not die.

Margaret Wilson
Lexington, KY

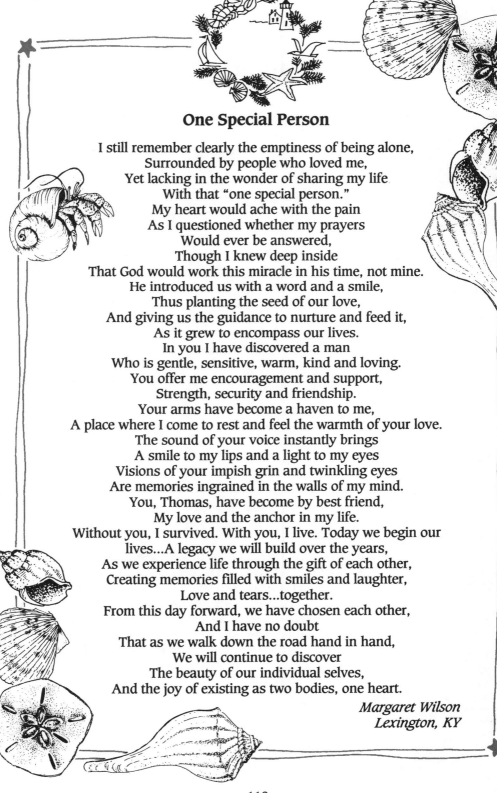

One Special Person

I still remember clearly the emptiness of being alone,
Surrounded by people who loved me,
Yet lacking in the wonder of sharing my life
With that "one special person."
My heart would ache with the pain
As I questioned whether my prayers
Would ever be answered,
Though I knew deep inside
That God would work this miracle in his time, not mine.
He introduced us with a word and a smile,
Thus planting the seed of our love,
And giving us the guidance to nurture and feed it,
As it grew to encompass our lives.
In you I have discovered a man
Who is gentle, sensitive, warm, kind and loving.
You offer me encouragement and support,
Strength, security and friendship.
Your arms have become a haven to me,
A place where I come to rest and feel the warmth of your love.
The sound of your voice instantly brings
A smile to my lips and a light to my eyes
Visions of your impish grin and twinkling eyes
Are memories ingrained in the walls of my mind.
You, Thomas, have become by best friend,
My love and the anchor in my life.
Without you, I survived. With you, I live. Today we begin our
lives...A legacy we will build over the years,
As we experience life through the gift of each other,
Creating memories filled with smiles and laughter,
Love and tears...together.
From this day forward, we have chosen each other,
And I have no doubt
That as we walk down the road hand in hand,
We will continue to discover
The beauty of our individual selves,
And the joy of existing as two bodies, one heart.

Margaret Wilson
Lexington, KY

119

Food for the Soul

The first man I ever fell in love with is my Dad! When I look back at my childhood, I remember good things. My mom and dad always taught my two brothers and me respect, inspiration, trust and most importantly love. They encouraged us to go beyond our gifts and strive for our goals. My dad is a gentle soul, always has been. But he had one problem. A problem none of us spoke about. He is an alcoholic. I watched this man I love die inside, his spirit drifting away. He became very ill with congestive heart failure to the point that he almost died. I remember so well the day, trying to tell my father he was ill because of alcoholism. He became very stoic but with love, encouragement and especially his own courage, he entered an alcoholic treatment center. It was the hardest thing I have ever had to do, to leave him there. As I drove home, I wasn't sure it was the right course of action. But it was. As the days and weeks rolled by, my father was becoming a new man. The man I remember loving so much! It has been over a year now in which my father has been sober. He has made such great strides and I am forever proud of him. He heads AA meetings and is on a medical board for alcoholics. My dad has blossomed into a new man. A man I remember as a little girl, as I said, the first man I fell in love with! This story is for you, Dad. I love you.

Cynthia Overstreet
Dallas, OR

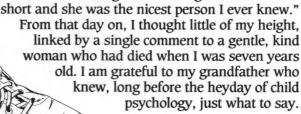

At five feet tall, I am, and always have been, the shortest member of my family. When I was a child (and even today) my height was the subject of many comments. One day my grandfather took me aside and said, "Don't mind being short. Your grandmother was short and she was the nicest person I ever knew." From that day on, I thought little of my height, linked by a single comment to a gentle, kind woman who had died when I was seven years old. I am grateful to my grandfather who knew, long before the heyday of child psychology, just what to say.

Eileen Jolls
Erie, PA

Laughter is brightest
where food is best.

Irish Proverb

Herbs

Skinny Minis

SKINNY MINI

Low-Fat Shrimp Dip

Deborah Peters
Breinigsville, PA

8 oz. pkg. cream cheese, fat-free
4 1/2 oz. can tiny shrimp,
    drained and rinsed
1 T. horseradish
1 T. mayonnaise, low-fat or
    fat-free

dash of Worcestershire
    sauce
dash bottled lemon juice
1/2 c. cocktail sauce

In a medium bowl, combine the cream cheese, shrimp, horseradish, mayonnaise, Worcestershire sauce and lemon juice; blend well. Refrigerate at least one hour. Put in a serving bowl, shaping the dip into a ball. Pour the cocktail sauce over the ball (or around it). Serve with reduced fat or no-fat crackers. Serves 6 to 8. (46 calories, and no fat per serving)

Mexican Dip

Deborah Peters
Breinigsville, PA

Serve with fat-free tortilla chips or fat-free pita bread wedges.

2- 15 oz. cans turkey chili
    with beans
16 oz. container fat-free
    sour cream
12 oz. jar salsa

1 1/2 c. cheddar cheese,
    fat-free
1 1/4 oz. pkg. taco
    seasoning

Layer the chili, sour cream, salsa, cheddar cheese and taco seasoning (only use 1/3 of the package) in order, in a pie plate. Heat, covered, in the microwave for 5 minutes or until the cheese is thoroughly melted. Serves 8. (149 calories, 1 gram fat per serving)

Tortilla Roll-Ups

Jackie Kelly
Florissant, MO

8 oz. pkg. light cream cheese
1/3 c. chunky salsa
1/4 c. green onion, chopped

1/2 t. garlic salt
1/2 t. chili powder
12 flour tortillas

Beat cream cheese until smooth; add salsa, onion, garlic salt, and chili powder. Mix well. Spread 1 to 2 tablespoons on each tortilla. Roll up jellyroll fashion and place seam side down on tray. Cover and chill 2 hours. Slice into 1 1/2-inch pieces and serve with salsa and guacamole.

Artichoke Dip

Janice Ertola
Martinez, CA

14 oz. can artichoke hearts
   in water, drained
1/2 c. fat-free mayonnaise

1/2 c. fat-free
   parmesan cheese
1 bag baked tortilla chips

Chop up artichoke hearts. Mix together artichoke hearts, mayonnaise and cheese. Spread into quiche dish. Bake at 350 degrees for 20 to 30 minutes. The top will be lightly browned. Serve with tortilla chips. Serves 8.

Fresh Herbs-n-Garlic Dip

DiAnn Voegele
Mascoutah, IL

Serve with fresh vegetables or chips.

1 c. low-fat sour cream
1 c. low-fat mayonnaise
2 T. parsley
2 T. chives

1 T. thyme
1 T. rosemary
2 T. garlic chives
1 clove garlic, crushed

Mix in glass bowl sour cream, mayonnaise, herbs and garlic. Cover and refrigerate overnight. Makes 2 cups.

SKINNY MINIS

Piña Colada Fruit Dip

Angie Yanchik
Cherry Hill, NJ

This is my favorite recipe using skim milk and fat-free sour cream... absolutely sinful and only 2 grams of fat per 1/2 cup serving!

8 oz. can crushed, pineapple, undrained
3 oz pkg. instant coconut cream pudding and pie filling

3/4 c. skim milk
1/2 c. fat-free sour cream

Combine all ingredients in blender and refrigerate several hours before serving. Can be served in "dip type" dish with assorted fresh fruits, or in a half cantaloupe or half pineapple.

Low-Fat Fruit Dip

Deborah Peters
Breinigsville, PA

Serve with fresh fruit and/or chunks of angel food or pound cake.

1 large container light, whipped topping
1/4 c. reduced-fat peanut butter

Blend the peanut butter into the container of whipped topping. Refrigerate for 1 hour before serving. Serves 8. (37 calories, 2 grams fat per serving)

Spinach Dip

Jennifer Broski
Chula Vista, CA

12 oz. container non-fat
    cottage cheese
1 T. lemon juice
1 c. non-fat mayonnaise
8 oz. can water chestnuts,
    drained and chopped

1 T. onion, grated
10 oz. pkg. chopped
    spinach, thawed
    and drained
1/4 c. dry vegetable
    soup mix

Blend cottage cheese in mixing bowl until smooth consistency.
Place in medium-sized bowl. Add spinach and remaining ingredients to cottage cheese mixture, stirring well. Serve with fresh
vegetables or non-fat crackers. Makes about 3 cups.

Dream Cheese

Barbara Hamilton
Victorville, CA

12 oz. plain, non-fat
    yogurt
2 automatic coffeemaker
    coffee filters

1 large tea-type
    strainer*

Place coffee filters (doubled) inside strainer. Rest the strainer on the
top of a 2-cup bowl. Spoon yogurt into the coffee filters and gently
stir. Place in refrigerator overnight. The excess liquid will drain into
the bowl leaving a delicious cream cheese substitute. Scoop out the
"Dream Cheese" and store in a covered container in the refrigerator.
Makes approximately 1 cup.

*Must hold at least 1 1/2 cups. There are commercially produced
yogurt strainers available in specialty cooking shops. I find
that the coffee filters, doubled, work equally well.

Note: Pat Husek of St. Joseph, MI sent a similar recipe
along with this suggestion: Mix the yogurt cheese
with your choice of shredded or chopped vegetables
and herbs. Experiment: radishes, carrots and
onions, chives, dill, garlic, salt and pepper!
Keeps in fridge three days.

Skinny Mini

Clandestine Dip

Judy Kelly
Florissant, MO

I got this recipe from a friend about twenty years ago and try to bring it out every summer when the tomatoes are at their peak. It is a very light beginning to a summer barbecue and contains very little oil. This should be made the day you are to serve it, not the day before.

2 large tomatoes, chopped
3 to 4 green onions, chopped
1 1/2 T. wine vinegar
1 t. salt
1 small can green chiles, chopped

3 T. olive oil
   (or salad oil)
1 small can black
   olives, chopped
1 t. garlic salt

Mix above ingredients all together. Refrigerate for several hours. Stir before serving. Serve with tortilla chips.

Hummus Spread

Jamey Kelley
Florissant, MO

A delicious middle-Eastern spread...Serve with warm pita bread cut into triangles!

2 cans garbanzos (chick peas), drained
1/2 c. tahini* (sesame paste)
1/3 c. warm water
1/3 c. extra virgin olive oil
juice of 2 to 3 lemons
4 or more garlic cloves
1 1/2 t. salt
2 t. cumin
fresh ground black pepper, to taste

Combine chick peas, tahini, water, olive oil, and lemon juice in food processor until smooth and creamy. Add garlic, salt, cumin and pepper; blend. Refrigerate until ready to use.

*Found in most health food stores.

Cherry Crab Spread

Dale Evans
Frankfort, MI

8 oz. pkg. light cream
   cheese, softened
2 T. 1% milk
7 oz. can crabmeat, drained
   and flaked
1 T. green onion, chopped

1/4 t. seasoned salt
1/8 t. garlic powder
1/2 c. dried cherries,
   snipped
parsley for garnish

In a small bowl, beat cream cheese and milk until fluffy. Add crab-meat, green onions, seasoned salt and garlic powder; mix well. Stir in cherries. Chill. Before serving garnish with parsley. Serve with crackers or raw vegetables. (Serving size: 2 tablespoons, 73 calories, 3.5 grams fat)

Spanish Bean Dip

Barbara Bargdill
Gooseberry Patch
Personal Shopper

1 17-oz. can non-fat
   refried beans
1/4 c. low-fat or non-fat
   sour cream
4 scallions, sliced
1/4 c. mild canned green
   chilies, diced

1 t. chili powder
4 oz. part skim
   mozzarella cheese,
   grated
1/4 c. low-fat or non-
   fat plain yogurt

Mix all ingredients together in a saucepan until well blended. Heat gently over medium heat for 10 minutes, stirring often. Serve hot or at room temperature with non-fat tortilla chips or vegetables.

Marinated Broccoli and Mushroom Appetizer

Jeanne Calkins
Midland, MI

I have been serving this recipe at family functions for the past eight years. It is one my father-in-law looks forward to at our Thanksgiving and Christmas dinners. It is very tasty and very low calorie!

1 T. lemon juice
2 t. tarragon vinegar
1 t. Dijon mustard
1 T. plus 1 t. olive oil
2 t. fresh parsley, minced
1/4 c. fresh chives or
   2 chopped scallions

1/2 t. each: salt and
   fennel seed
1/8 t. fresh ground pepper
2 c. halved mushrooms,
   blanched
1 1/2 c. broccoli florets,
   blanched

In measuring cup or small bowl, combine lemon juice, vinegar, and mustard. Gradually add oil, stirring constantly, until mixture becomes thick and creamy; add parsley, chives or scallions, salt, fennel, and pepper and mix well. Set aside. In a medium bowl (non-metallic) combine mushrooms, broccoli, and dressing, toss to lightly coat the veggies. Cover with plastic wrap and refrigerate overnight. It is very important to let set at least 10 hours so the flavors may mellow and the veggies soak up all of the flavor. Yields 4 servings.

Fried Green Tomatoes

1 green tomato, sliced
1 egg, beaten
1/4 c. seasoned Italian bread crumbs

2 T. Parmesan cheese
1 T. olive oil
slice of fresh lemon

Dip tomato slices into egg, then dredge in mixture of bread crumbs and cheese. In non-stick skillet, saute in oil over medium heat, turning until slices are tender and both sides are browned. Sprinkle with fresh lemon, if desired.
Serves one or two.

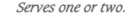

Quick Quenchers

Quick Quenchers

Fat-Free Cappuccino Mix

Dora Humble
Chula Vista, CA

I use the cappuccino mix to give as gifts all year long. I divide the mix into small jam jars, with the serving instructions tied with a colorful ribbon around the lid.

6 T. plus 2 t. instant espresso coffee powder
1/2 c. plus 2 t. sugar
3 T. plus 1 t. unsweetened cocoa powder
1 T. vanilla extract powder
1 1/4 c. fat-free coffee creamer

Stir all ingredients together and store tightly covered in a medium bowl. Makes 10 servings. Serving instructions: For each cup of cappuccino, measure 4 tablespoons mix into coffee mug and stir in 6 ounces of boiling water.

Coffee Nog a la Mode

Barbara Bargdill
Gooseberry Patch Personal Shopper

1 c. coffee (strong), brewed
1/2 c. frozen egg substitute,
**   thawed**
1/4 c. sugar

3 c. skim milk
1 1/2 c. vanilla non-fat
**   frozen yogurt**
1/4 t. ground nutmeg

Combine coffee, egg substitute, and sugar in a large saucepan; stir well. Gradually add milk, stirring well. Cook over low heat until thoroughly heated, stirring constantly (do not boil). Pour 3/4 cup coffee mixture into each of 6 mugs. Top each with 1/4 cup frozen yogurt, sprinkle evenly with ground nutmeg. Serve immediately. Yield: 6 servings.

Homemade Instant Hot Chocolate

Diann Fox
Lewisberry, PA

This mix has no preservatives or artificial colorings.

4 c. instant non-fat dry milk	1 c. sugar
3/4 c. sweetened cocoa mix	1/8 t. salt

Combine all ingredients, stirring well. Store in a tightly covered 2-quart container in a cool, dry place. To make a cup of hot chocolate: Place 3 1/2 tablespoons of hot chocolate mix in 1 cup of boiling water and stir. For a richer hot chocolate, use hot milk instead of water.

Creamy Kiwi Freeze

Cynthia Coffman
Lewisberry, PA

1 kiwi, peeled	2 T. honey
1/2 c. vanilla non-fat frozen yogurt	1/2 c. seltzer or club soda, chilled

About 5 minutes before serving cut kiwi in quarters. In blender at high speed, blend kiwi, frozen yogurt and remaining ingredients 1 minute. Pour into 2 chilled glasses. Makes 2 servings.

Tropical Magic

Cynthia Coffman
Lewisburg, PA

1 small mango
8 oz. can pineapple chunks in unsweetened
    pineapple juice
1 c. seltzer or club soda, chilled
3 ice cubes
1/4 t. coconut extract

About 10 minutes before serving, peel mango and cut into bite-size pieces. In blender at high speed, blend mango, pineapple with its juice and remaining ingredients for 1 minute. Pour into 2 chilled glasses. Makes 2 servings.

Quick Quenchers

California Lemon Cocktail

Pat Akers
Stanton, CA

Here is a healthy drink (and a way for all of us Californians with lemon trees to use the bountiful lemons these trees produce)!

4 lemons
3 1/2 c. orange-pineapple juice
1/2 c. low-calorie cranberry
juice cocktail

1 T. honey
1/2 c. fresh or thawed
frozen strawberries

Thinly slice 1 lemon and set the slices aside. Squeeze the juice from the remaining lemons. In a large pitcher, combine the lemon juice, orange-pineapple juice, cranberry juice and honey. In a small bowl, use a fork or pastry blender to crush the strawberries until they resemble a coarse puree. Stir the strawberries into the juice mixture and add the lemon slices. Refrigerate until ready to serve. Makes 6 cups.

Yogurt Smoothie

Nancie Gensler
Walnut Creek, CA

You'll need a blender for this recipe. It makes a nutritious, low-fat lunch. Delicious and very filling.

1 small carton low-fat yogurt with
fruit on bottom
1 banana (any combination of berries,
peaches, strawberries, or any soft fruit
can be included or substituted)*
1/2 c. fruit juice (orange, pineapple, etc.)
3 ice cubes

Put in blender and blend until smooth.

*You can use over-ripened fruit that you might be tempted to toss.

Treat yourself to a bouquet of fresh flowers!

Fruit Smoothie

Carole Brooks
Chula Vista, CA

2 to 3 T. non-fat yogurt
4 oz. orange juice
ice cubes

fresh or frozen strawberries
   or fruit of your choice
1 banana

Blend all ingredients in electric blender. Enjoy!

Apple-Banana Shake

Heather Hood
Bloomington, MN

A frothy, refreshing drink!

1 small banana
5 to 6 ice cubes

1 c. granny smith apple juice
   (no sugar added)

Blend all ingredients in blender.

"Egg" Nog

Paula Zsiray
Logan, UT

This is great and there is no raw egg to worry about. My kids love it. If you are so inclined, it also "spikes" well! I like it better than the old-fashioned egg nog with real eggs.

1 3 oz. pkg. vanilla instant pudding*
1/3 c. sugar (or equivalent of sugar substitute)
8 c. milk, low-fat or skim
2 t. vanilla
1/2 t. nutmeg (up to 1 t. if you
   really like it)

In a large bowl, mix all ingredients well. Serve chilled. Keeps well in refrigerator.

*Also: French vanilla or fat-free vanilla instant pudding.

Healthy Sport Drink

Barbara Truax
St. Louis, MO

1/2 c. orange juice
1/2 c. pineapple juice
1/2 small banana

4 fresh strawberries
several ice cubes

Combine in a blender and whirl a few seconds. Pour into a tall iced tea glass and garnish with a sprig of fresh mint. Serves 1.

Banana Malts

Julie Brose
Granada Hills, CA

Here is a healthy, low-fat treat that both kids and adults love. Keep a supply of frozen bananas on hand. This is a great way to make use of bananas that are getting old; just peel them, pop them into plastic sandwich bag and tuck them into your freezer. There is a variety of wonderful fat-free frozen yogurts and ice creams in the grocery stores today...the banana adds a richness to the malt without adding the fat.

2 frozen bananas broken into pieces
1 heaping T. malt powder
1 c. cold 1% or non-fat milk
flavorings*
6 scoops low-fat or no-fat ice cream

Whirl all these ingredients in the blender until smooth, adding a little more milk if needed. Makes 4 servings. To make a fancy, impressive serving, put in a malt glass or tall glass with colorful straw and garnish with cherry on top! (To make a shake, just eliminate the malt powder.)

*Add whatever ingredients you would like to flavor malt:

2 heaping T. chocolate milk powder
    and/or 4 T. chocolate syrup
1/4 t. peppermint extract
handful of fresh berries
1/4 c. any flavor fruit preserves (be creative!)

Strawberry Colada

Christine Mattox
Tucker, GA

I drink a lot of water before and during exercise. BUT...when I've completed a rigorous workout and finished my "cool-down," I like to reward myself with a luscious, low-fat beverage.

6 oz. can pineapple juice
1/4 c. non-alcoholic piña colada mix
2 c. fat-free vanilla frozen yogurt
1 c. fresh or frozen strawberries (no sugar added)

Combine all ingredients in a blender and blend until smooth. Pour into a tall glass and garnish with fresh berries if desired. Yields 4- 3/4 cup servings. Approximately 150 calories each serving, less than 1 gram of fat.

Fat-Free Float

Christine Mattox
Tucker, GA

This is very satisfying if you have a sweet tooth!!

glass of your favorite diet soda*
scoop of fat-free vanilla frozen yogurt

Pour a glass of the diet soda and add a scoop of yogurt. Plunk in a straw, sip and relax.

*Try a new flavor...peach, orange or root beer!

Sun Tea

Nancy Campbell
Bellingham, WA

12 tea bags
gallon of tap water
1/8 c. lemon juice

sugar to taste
1 t. raspberry syrup
mint sprigs

Make a pot of sun tea with tea bags and water. Leave out in the sun all day. (We put our jar of tea up on our roof!) Remove bags, add lemon juice, and sugar. Mix well. Add garnish of thin slice of lemon, sprig of mint or raspberry syrup. Serve over ice.

Veggies, fresh fruit and edible flowers make delightful garnishes. They're pleasing to the taste as well as to the eye!

Rise & Shine...
Muffins
& More

Blueberry Whole Wheat Yogurt Muffins

Diane Donato
West Chicago, IL

This is my most-requested recipe. It is a favorite at my office, where they don't even know it is a low-fat recipe.

1 c. all-purpose flour
1 c. whole wheat flour
1/3 c. sugar
1/4 t. salt
2 t. baking soda
1/4 c. unsweetened
   orange juice
1 egg

8 oz. carton of vanilla
   low-fat yogurt
1 t. vanilla extract
2 T. vegetable oil
1 c. fresh or frozen
   blueberries, thawed
1 T. sugar

Preheat oven to 400 degrees. Spray 12 muffin cups with cooking spray. Combine the first five ingredients in a large bowl. (Do not pack flour into measuring cups! Stir it in its storage container and then scoop it into a measuring cup, leveling off with a flat spatula.) Make a well in the center of the dry ingredient mixture. Combine orange juice and the next four ingredients in a separate bowl; stir well. Add to dry ingredients, stirring until just moistened. Gently fold in blueberries. Spoon batter into muffin cups, filling almost to the top. Sprinkle one tablespoon of sugar evenly onto muffins. Bake for 18 minutes or until golden. Remove from pans immediately. Cool on wire rack. Yields 11 to 12 muffins.

Carrot-Applesauce Muffins

*Pat Husek
St. Joseph, MI*

Tastes like carrot cake!

2 1/2 c. all-purpose flour
3/4 c. sugar
2 1/2 t. baking powder
1/4 t. baking soda
1/4 t. salt
1 1/2 t. ground cinnamon
1/2 t. ground ginger
1/4 t. ground nutmeg
1/8 t. ground cloves
1 1/2 c. carrots, shredded
1/2 c. non-fat plain yogurt
1 large egg, beaten
1/4 c. oil
1 t. vanilla
1 c. unsweetened applesauce
1 T. flaked coconut

Preheat oven to 400 degrees. Lightly grease regular-sized muffin tin. Combine dry ingredients. Add shredded carrots and blend. Stir together yogurt, egg, oil, vanilla and applesauce. Stir the liquid ingredients into the dry ingredients just until moistened. Spoon into tins. Sprinkle top with coconut. Bake 20 to 22 minutes. Makes 12 muffins. (Each muffin: 232 calories, 5.34 grams fat, 1.86 grams fiber)

Three-Grain Honey and Fruit Muffins

*Pat Husek
St. Joseph, MI*

1 c. whole wheat flour
1/2 c. all-purpose flour
1/2 c. stone-ground rye flour, unsifted
3 t. baking powder
1/2 t. baking soda
1/2 t. salt
1/2 c. old-fashioned rolled oats
2 c. non-fat buttermilk
1/2 c. honey
2 egg whites, beaten
1 c. mixed dried fruits, or dates, chopped; or raisins

Preheat oven to 400 degrees. Lightly grease muffin tin. Mix together dry ingredients. Mix together liquid ingredients. Add liquid to dry mixture. Stir in fruit. Bake 20 to 25 minutes. Cool 1 minute and remove to rack. Makes 12 muffins. (151 calories, less than 1 gram fat, 3.3 grams fiber)

Pumpkin-Oat Bran Muffins

Carol Young
South Whitley, IN

These are wonderful on the go. They're healthy and yummy, and they freeze well.

1 1/2 c. unprocessed oat bran
1/2 c. brown sugar, firmly
   packed
1/2 c. all-purpose flour
2 t. baking powder
1 t. pumpkin pie spice
1/2 t. salt

1 c. pumpkin, cooked
   and mashed
1/2 c. skim milk
2 egg whites, lightly
   beaten
2 T. vegetable oil

Combine first 6 ingredients in a large bowl; stir well. Make a well in center of mixture. Combine pumpkin and next 3 ingredients; stir well. Add to dry ingredients, stirring just until moistened. Spoon into muffin pans coated with cooking spray, filling three-fourths full. Bake at 425 degrees for 20 minutes. Remove from pans immediately; serve warm or at room temperature. Yields 1 dozen (about 140 calories each).

Apple-Date Muffins

Glenda Hill
Columbus, OH

You can make these muffins ahead of time and freeze until ready to use. They're high in fiber and tasty, too.

1 c. whole wheat flour
3/4 c. oats
1/2 t. salt
3 t. baking powder
1 medium apple, grated*
1 c. milk

1 egg, lightly beaten
3 T. oil
3 T. honey, or apple juice
   concentrate for sugar-free
1/2 c. pitted dates, cut in
   tiny pieces (or use blender)

Preheat oven to 400 degrees. Combine dry ingredients. In separate bowl combine wet ingredients and fruit. Make a well in the dry ingredients and add wet ingredients. Stir just until moist. Spoon into oiled muffin cups and bake 15 to 20 minutes. Makes 12 muffins.

*Grate apple just before using to prevent browning.

Spicy Blueberry Muffins

Glenda Hill
Columbus, OH

1 c. whole wheat flour
1/2 c. quick oats
1 1/4 t. baking powder
1/4 t. salt
1/2 t. cinnamon
1/4 t. nutmeg

1/4 c. honey
1 egg, lightly beaten
1/2 c. milk
2 T. oil
1/2 c. fresh blueberries

Clean blueberries and set aside. Combine dry ingredients. In separate bowl combine wet ingredients. Add wet ingredients to dry ingredients, stir until moist. Add blueberries and stir lightly. Spoon into oiled muffin cups, filling 2/3 full. Bake for 15 minutes at 400 degrees. Makes 12 muffins.

Cinnamon Muffins

Glenda Hill
Columbus, OH

These muffins smell wonderful as they bake! The wonderful aroma fills your whole house.

1 1/2 c. whole wheat flour
1 1/2 tsp. baking powder
1 1/2 t. cinnamon
1/2 t. baking soda
1/4 t. salt
1 egg

1 c. buttermilk
1/4 c. honey, or 1/2 c.
    apple juice concentrate
3 T. applesauce
2 T. oil

Sift together dry ingredients. In separate bowl combine wet ingredients. Make a well in dry ingredients and add wet ingredients. Stir until moist. Spoon into oiled muffin tins. Bake at 400 degrees for 20 minutes. Makes 12 muffins.

No-Fat Banana Muffins

Kathy Grashoff
Ft. Wayne, IN

1/2 c. applesauce
2 eggs, or egg substitute
1 t. baking powder
1/2 t. salt
1/2 t. cinnamon

1 c. bananas, mashed
1/2 c. sugar
1 3/4 c. flour
1/2 t. baking soda
1/2 t. nutmeg

Preheat oven to 350 degrees. Spray muffin tin with non-stick cooking spray. Combine all the ingredients and mix well. Pour into 12 muffin cups. Bake for 20 minutes. Delicious when warm.
(Per muffin: 116 calories, no fat)

Low-Fat Chocolate Muffins

Mary Shrank
Santa Clara, CA

1 c. plus 2 T. all-purpose flour
3/4 c. granulated sugar
3/4 c. unsweetened cocoa
1 1/2 t. baking powder
1/2 t. baking soda

1/4 t. salt
3 large egg whites
2 t. vanilla
1/2 c. prune puree*
3/4 c. water

Position rack in center of oven, preheat oven to 350 degrees. Coat 12 muffin tins with non-stick cooking spray. In a large mixing bowl, combine flour, sugar, cocoa, baking powder, baking soda and salt. Blend well using a wire whisk. Make a well in the center. In a separate bowl, whisk egg whites with vanilla, prune puree and water. Add to flour mixture. Stir just until blended. Do not over-mix. Spoon into prepared muffin tins. Bake 25 minutes or until a toothpick comes out clean. Cool on wire rack for 15 minutes before removing from pan. Makes 12 muffins.

*In a food processor container combine 1 1/3 cups dried pitted prunes, 6 tablespoons hot water and 1 teaspoon vanilla. Pulse on and off until fruit is finely chopped. Cool before using. Makes about 1 cup.

Pineapple Plus Muffins

Kathy Epperly
Wichita, KS

whole-grain English muffin　　**crushed pineapple with juice**
low-fat cream cheese　　**cinnamon**

Spread English muffin with low-fat cream cheese. Spoon crushed pineapple on both slices and sprinkle with cinnamon. Broil for 4 minutes. Serves 1.

Basic Whole-Grain Muffins

Mel Wolk
St. Peters, MO

I have one basic whole-grain muffin recipe that I use for most muffin snacks. It makes a lot, so I divide the batter and add fruit, nuts, raisins, oats, even peanut butter, and freeze an assortment for later.

6 c. whole wheat flour　　**1 1/2 t. salt**
2 T. baking powder　　**3 eggs**
3/4 c. brown sugar or honey　　**9 T. butter or margarine,**
1 T. cinnamon　　**melted**
1/2 t. ground cloves　　**3 c. milk**

Mix dry ingredients. Combine wet ingredients and add to the dry mixture. Stir until just moistened. Fill greased muffin tins about half full and bake at 375 degrees for about 15 minutes. Makes 36 to 40 large yummy muffins.

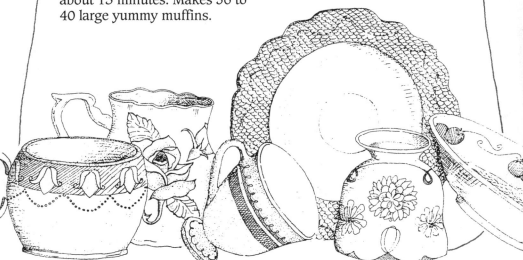

Apricot Waffles

Janice Ertola
Martinez, CA

This is good served with an assortment of fresh fruit.

12 frozen waffles (or make your own)
6 T. light apricot preserves
8 oz. container non-fat vanilla yogurt
2 t. honey
2 c. strawberries sliced

Heat waffles according to package. Spread 6 waffles with 1 tablespoon preserves; top each with a plain waffle. In a small bowl, combine yogurt and honey and blend well. To serve: Place 1 waffle sandwich on each plate, top with yogurt mixture and strawberries. Serve at once. Makes 6 servings.

Fruit "Sundaes"

Kathy Epperly
Wichita, KS

3 c. chilled fruit, chopped or sliced
8 oz. non-fat, or plain low-fat yogurt
2 t. ground cinnamon

Dish fruit into 4 chilled dishes. Top with a dollop of yogurt. Sprinkle with cinnamon. Serves 4.

Fruit possibilities: apples, raisins, fresh or canned pears, kiwis, red grapes, naval orange sections, bananas, kiwis, mangos, papayas, fresh blackberries, nectarines and/or peaches, fresh strawberries

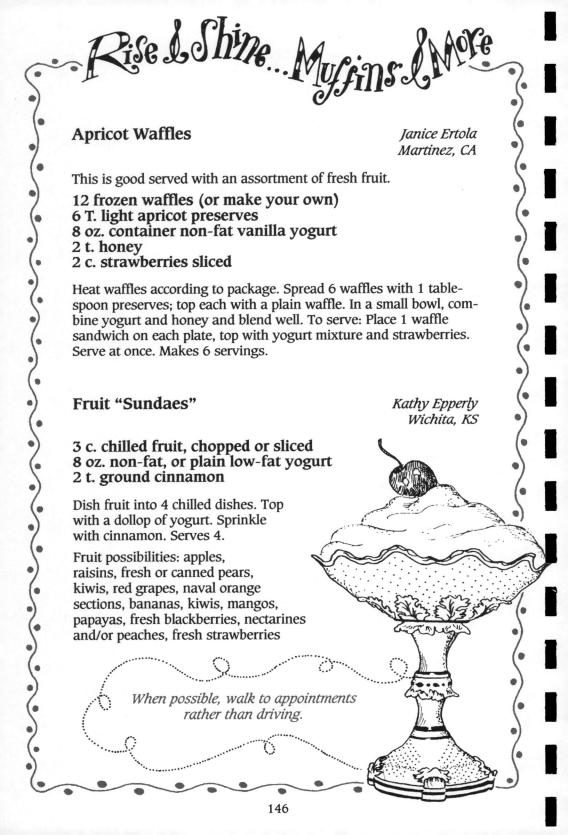

When possible, walk to appointments rather than driving.

Fruit Salad Bagels

Kathy Epperly
Wichita, KS

**non-fat or low-fat cream cheese
   or cottage cheese
bagel**

**cinnamon
fresh fruit**

Spread non-fat or low-fat cream cheese or cottage cheese on toasted bagel and sprinkle with cinnamon. Top with thin slices of banana, honeydew and/or peaches. Serves 1.

Breakfast Banana Shake

Pat Akers
Stanton, CA

This breakfast shake not only gives me a boost of morning energy, but has a great flavor.

**2 bananas, sliced
2 c. skim milk
2 c. non-fat vanilla yogurt**

**1/2 c. pineapple juice
1 T. honey**

In a blender process the bananas, milk, yogurt, juice and honey until smooth. Serve immediately. Makes 4 servings.

Baked French Toast

Jo Baker
Litchfield, IL

Serve with fresh fruit.

**1 c. maple syrup or substitute
1 loaf French bread
3 eggs
3 egg whites**

**1 1/2 c. skim milk
2 t. vanilla
3/4 t. nutmeg**

Lightly spray a large baking dish with vegetable oil. Pour syrup into the dish. Slice bread into 8-2" slices and place them in the syrup. In a separate bowl, combine eggs, egg whites, milk, vanilla and 1/4 teaspoon nutmeg; beat very well. Pour egg mixture over bread, pressing bread down to absorb batter. Refrigerate, covered, overnight. Preheat oven to 350 degrees. Sprinkle remaining nutmeg over bread. Bake for 40 to 45 minutes, until golden. Serves 8.

Sunshine Breakfast

Jo Baker
Litchfield, IL

A very healthy, quick breakfast. Saves time in the morning.

2 c. corn flakes	1 t. cinnamon
1/2 c. bran flakes	1 t. light brown sugar
1/2 c. quick oats	1/2 c. golden raisins
1/3 c. apple juice	1/2 c. other dried fruit of your choice (berries work well)

Preheat oven to 300 degrees. Combine all ingredients, except dried fruits; mix well. Spread mixture onto a large cookie sheet. Bake for 30 minutes, until lightly browned. Add dried fruits and combine. Cool; store in airtight tin. Serves 4.

Fruit Sauce for Pancakes

Diann Fox
Lewisberry, PA

Delicious! Your family won't miss sugary pancake syrups!

2 c. fresh or frozen fruit (blueberries, peaches, cherries, etc.)	1 T. cornstarch
1/4 c. sugar or sugar to taste	1 1/2 c. cold water

Place fruit and sugar in a 2-quart saucepan. Mix cornstarch into cold water and add to fruit. Heat over medium heat, stirring frequently, until mixture thickens (about 5 to 10 minutes). Serve hot over pancakes or waffles.

Quiche without the Crust

Kathy Grashoff
Ft. Wayne, IN

4 slices bacon, diced
1 c. reduced-fat Swiss
  cheese, shredded
1/3 c. green onion, chopped
1/4 c. green pepper, diced
4 oz. can mushrooms, drained or
  1/2 c. fresh mushrooms, sliced

2 1/4 c. skim milk
1 c. "light" biscuit
  baking mix
2 eggs, beaten well
1/4 t. pepper

Preheat oven to 400 degrees. Dice bacon onto a microwave tray. Cover with paper towel and cook on high power for 3 minutes; drain. Spray a 9" pie plate with non-stick cooking spray. Sprinkle bacon pieces, shredded cheese, onion, green pepper and mushrooms over the pie plate. Beat remaining ingredients, in the blender or with a mixer, until smooth. Pour into pie. Bake for 30 minutes or until eggs have set. Makes 8 servings. (135 calories, 5 grams fat per serving)

Everyday Granola Cereal

Yvonne Van Brimmer
Lompoc, CA

6 c. rolled oats
1 c. unsweetened coconut
1 c. wheat germ
1 c. barley flakes

1 c. sunflower seeds
1 c. nuts, chopped
1 c. wheat or oat bran

In a large bowl mix all the above ingredients. In a four-cup, microwave-safe bowl, heat for 3 minutes on high the following:

1/4 c. canola oil
1 c. honey or maple syrup

1/2 c. water
2 t. vanilla or almond extract

Pour the heated liquid over the mixed grains and flakes. Stir to coat completely. Spread evenly on cookie sheets. Bake at 325 degrees for 30 minutes, stirring every 10 minutes. Remove and cool. After cooling you may add 2 cups of raisins or other chopped dried fruit.
Yields about 14 cups.

Raspberry French Toast

Deb Weiser
Gooseberry Patch Warehouse

3/4 c. fat-free egg
   substitute
1/2 t. vanilla
1/2 t. ground cinnamon
1/2 c. 1% milk or skim milk

8 slices "Texas toast" bread
   or French bread, sliced
2 c. raspberries or
   blackberries
1/4 c. low-cal maple syrup

In a medium bowl beat egg substitute, vanilla, cinnamon and milk. Dip bread on both sides. Fry on griddle with no-stick spray, using medium heat until brown. Top with berries and syrup.

Country Breakfast Casserole

Shirll Kosmal
Gooseberry Patch Warehouse

This is light, only 5 grams of fat per serving!

1 T. vegetable oil
4 small potatoes, diced
1 sweet red pepper, diced
1 green pepper, diced
1 small onion, minced
1 1/2 c. egg substitute
1 c. skim milk

2 T. flour
1/4 t. black pepper
4 oz. low-fat cheddar cheese,
   shredded
8 oz. pkg. meatless breakfast
   link sausage, chopped

Heat oil in medium skillet. Fry potatoes in oil until golden. Add peppers and onion. Mix egg substitute, milk, flour, black pepper, cheese and breakfast links in mixing bowl. Fold in hot potato mixture. Coat a 12" x 8" baking dish with vegetable cooking spray. Pour potato mixture into baking dish. Bake at 350 degrees for 45 minutes. Makes 8 servings.

Note: A small bag of frozen seasoned hash brown potatoes can be used instead of potatoes, onion and sweet peppers.

Treat yourself to the best mattress and cotton sheets your money can buy.

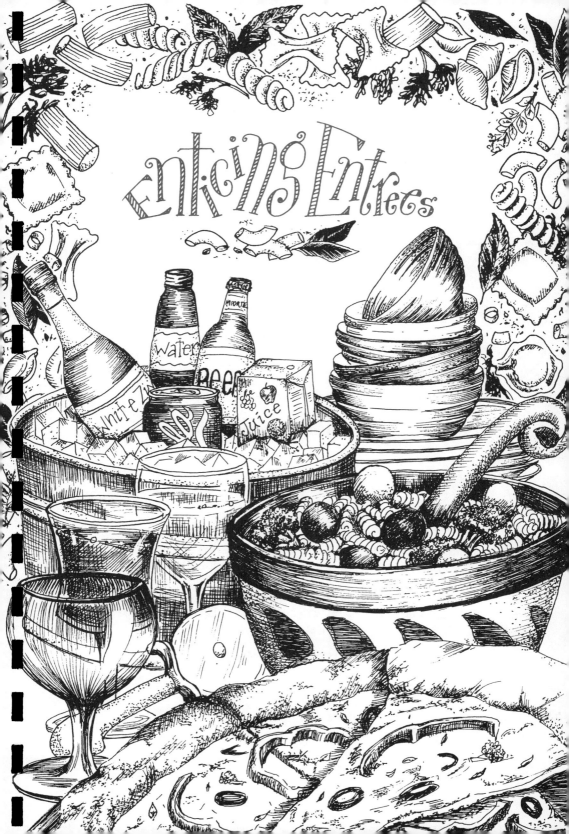

Enticing Entrees

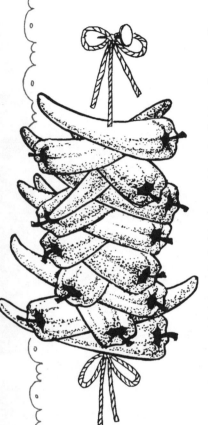

White Chili

Amy Schueddig
Arnold, MO

4 chicken breasts
1 T. olive oil
2 medium onions, chopped
4 cloves garlic, minced
2- 4 oz. cans mild green chilies,
    chopped
2 t. ground cumin
1 1/2 t. dried oregano, crumbled
1/4 t. cayenne pepper
1/4 t. ground red pepper
3-16 oz. cans white beans
5 c. chicken broth, de-fatted
3 c. (12 oz.) reduced-fat Monterey
    Jack cheese, shredded
no-fat sour cream
jalapeno peppers
salt and pepper to taste

Place chicken in a heavy saucepan. Add cold water to cover and bring to simmer. Cook until tender, about 15 minutes. Drain and cool. Remove skin and shred into bite-size pieces. Heat oil in same pot over medium/high heat. Add onions and sauté until translucent (about 10 minutes). Stir in garlic, then chilies, cumin, oregano, cayenne and red pepper. Sauté 2 minutes. Add undrained beans and broth and bring to boil. Reduce heat, add chicken and cheese until cheese melts. Serve immediately. Garnish with sour cream and jalapeno peppers, if desired. Makes 12 main dish servings.

A plate of fresh fruit
in your bedroom is perfect
for a late night snack.

Black Beans and Rice

Diann Fox
Lewisberry, PA

Serve with a salad and you have a quick, nutritious meal.

hot cooked rice, white or brown
15 to 20 oz. can black beans
1/2 t. beef bouillon
2 c. sharp or Monterey Jack cheese, shredded (you may substitute with cheese of your choice)

12 oz. jar garden-style salsa
8 oz. plain yogurt
2 T. green onions, chopped

In a 3-quart saucepan prepare rice according to package directions. In a 2-quart saucepan heat black beans, beef bouillon and green onions, on medium heat, until hot...but do not boil. To serve: layer on each plate about 1/2 cup of rice, then 1/4 to 1/2 cup black bean mix. Sprinkle cheese on top of the hot beans. Add about 3 tablespoons of salsa. Garnish with a spoonful of yogurt and chopped green onions. Each family member can adjust each layer to suit their individual tastes. Serves 4.

Waist-Watcher Taco Pie

Mary Warren
Auburn, MI

It seems we are always trying to think of ways to eat healthier these days, especially come winter, when we are less active and fewer fresh vegetables are available. This is a recipe my family and friends like. It tastes good and is good for you.

8 oz. pkg. refrigerator biscuits
1 lb. ground turkey
1 T. beef bouillon powder
2 T. onion, chopped
2 T. green pepper, chopped

salt and pepper to taste
3/4 c. tomato paste
3/4 c. water
1 pkg. taco seasoning
6 oz. no-fat cheese, grated

Make a crust with the biscuits in an 8" square pan or pie dish by pressing them down. Brown meat, add bouillon, veggies and salt and pepper. Heat until veggies are tender. Add tomato paste, water and seasonings. Layer with meat over the biscuits. Top with cheese. Bake at 400 degrees for 15 minutes. Serve with chopped tomatoes, lettuce and hot sauce. Makes 8 servings.

Chicken Nuggets

Janice Ertola
Martinez, CA

2 1/2 c. corn flakes, crushed
1 t. paprika
1/2 t. garlic powder
1/2 t. oregano leaves
1 egg white

1 lb. chicken breasts,
   skinless and
   boneless (cut into
   1" pieces)
honey or catsup

Heat oven to 425 degrees. Spray cookie sheet with non-stick cooking spray. In plastic bag, combine corn flakes, paprika, garlic powder and oregano. Shake to mix. Place egg white in shallow bowl, beat slightly. Dip chicken pieces in egg, then shake dipped chicken (about 6 pieces at a time) in cereal mixture to coat. Place on cookie sheet. Bake at 425 degrees for 15 to 20 minutes until chicken is no longer pink and coating is crisp. Serve with honey or catsup as a dip. Makes about 4 servings (about 20 nuggets).

Barbecued Teriyaki Chicken Breasts

Sharon Chelin
Sandy, OR

This recipe is fast and easy, and the meat is so tender and moist.

4 chicken breast halves, skinned and boned
3 T. sugar
1/3 c. light soy sauce
1/3 c. white cooking wine
1/2 t. ginger
2 garlic cloves, minced

Lightly pound chicken with meat mallet to flatten. Place in shallow dish. Combine remaining ingredients in a small bowl and stir until sugar has dissolved. Pour over chicken, cover; refrigerate 1 to 2 hours, turning several times. Drain chicken. Place chicken breasts over hot coals, cooking 3 to 5 minutes per side or until meat is no longer pink inside. Be sure to spray grill with non-stick cooking spray before grilling chicken. Serves 4.

Almond with Cantaloupe Chicken Sandwiches

Kathy Epperly
Wichita, KS

2 T. non-fat or low-fat
   plain yogurt
2 T. reduced calorie
   mayonnaise
1 clove garlic, minced
1/2 t. black pepper
1/8 t. cayenne pepper
1 c. cooked chicken breast, chopped

1 c. cantaloupe, diced
1/2 c. almonds
   chopped
1 T. lemon juice
4 whole-grain French
   rolls
4 large romaine
   lettuce leaves

Combine yogurt, mayonnaise, garlic, black pepper and cayenne pepper in a medium bowl. Stir in the chicken breast, cantaloupe, almonds and 1 tablespoon lemon juice. Halve the whole-grain French rolls and top with the romaine lettuce. Top with chicken melon salad and remaining roll half. Serves 4.

Lemon Baked Chicken

Jo Baker
Litchfield, IL

1/4 c. olive oil or vegetable oil
1/4 c. fresh lemon juice
1 garlic clove, crushed
1 medium fryer (2 1/2 to 3 lbs.),
   skinned and cut into
   serving pieces
parsley, chopped
1 t. paprika

Thoroughly mix oil, lemon juice and garlic. Arrange chicken in a casserole dish and brush each piece thoroughly with lemon-oil mixture. Cover and bake at 350 degrees until tender, 45 to 60 minutes. Baste chicken occasionally with lemon-oil mixture. Uncover for last 20 minutes of baking to allow chicken to brown. Sprinkle with chopped parsley and paprika. Serves 4 to 6.

Enticing Entrees

Tarragon Chicken

Judy Borecky
Escondido, CA

I make this all the time. You can serve this wonderful dish over rice or mashed potatoes (my husband's favorite).

2 T. flour
salt and pepper
2 or 3 chicken breast halves
2 t. olive oil
1/4 c. brandy
3/4 c. fresh tomato pulp,
    or tomatoes, finely diced

1 to 2 T. shallots, or onions,
    diced
1/4 c. fat-free liquid dairy
    creamer
1/2 c. canned chicken
    broth
1/2 t. tarragon (I use dried)

Place flour, along with salt and pepper to taste, in a paper bag. Put chicken breasts in bag, close top and shake to coat chicken. Sauté in olive oil (you may need a little non-stick cooking spray). When almost done, add brandy and light with a match; stand back (don't get burned). Take chicken out of pan and make sauce in the same pan. Put tomatoes through a food processor. Cook shallots in pan that you took the chicken out of; add the rest of the ingredients and cook on fairly high heat for about a minute. Return chicken to pan.

Makes 2 or 3 servings.

Note: For reduced fat, you may remove skin from chicken before cooking.

Spring Chickens

Herb-Coated Chicken

Theresa M. Nobuyuki
Laguna Hills, CA

4 small boneless, skinless
   chicken breasts
2 T. Dijon mustard
1 T. whole-grain mustard
2 egg yolks, lightly beaten
3 T. cream
salt and pepper

3 T. French tarragon,
   chopped (or coriander
   or Italian parsley)
1 c. dry white bread crumbs
flour for dusting
3 T. oil for cooking

Pat the chicken breasts dry. Mix the mustards, egg yolks and cream in a shallow bowl. Season with salt and black pepper. Combine bread crumbs and chopped herbs on a large plate or a piece of wax paper. Dip each chicken breast in flour to coat it on all sides, then in the mustard mixture, turning it to coat evenly. Drain off any excess, then turn the chicken in the crumb mixture until it is well coated. Cover the coated chicken breasts and place them in the refrigerator for at least 4 hours. During this time, the flavors will penetrate the meat and the coating will set. Heat oil in large, heavy non-stick fry pan. Cook the chicken for about 10 minutes on each side, until golden brown. To test that the meat is cooked, pierce the thickest part with a fine skewer. The juice should run clear. Serves 4.

Have friends over for casual dinners. What a wonderful way to try new recipes! Let everyone help.

Low-Fat Chicken Italiano

Jeannine English
Wylie, TX

4 boneless, skinless chicken breasts
1 bottle low-fat or non-fat Italian
   salad dressing
2 c. bread crumbs
1 clove garlic, finely minced
1 T. parmesan cheese
2 T. Italian herbs mixture (oregano, basil,
   marjoram, thyme, savory, rosemary
   and sage)
1 T. parsley flakes

Marinate chicken breasts overnight in the Italian
salad dressing in the refrigerator. Shake excess off
chicken breasts and then roll in bread crumb and
seasonings mix. Spray baking sheet lightly with
no-stick spray. Bake uncovered in 325 degree
oven for approximately 45 minutes. Serves 4.

Raspberry Salsa Chicken Fettuccine

Cheryl Parker
Portland, OR

6 chicken breasts, skinless and boneless
10 oz. jar raspberry salsa
fettuccine for 6 people
1/2 pt. fat-free sour cream

Sauté chicken breasts in non-stick frying pan
(use cooking spray if needed) until chicken begins
to turn golden brown on each side. At this
point you can finish in frying pan. Pour salsa
over chicken, cover and simmer until chicken is done or
place chicken in coated baking dish. Pour salsa over
and bake covered at 350 degrees for 20 to 30 minutes. Boil fettuccine. Serve chicken over fettuccine
with dollop of fat-free sour cream.

Vegetable "Grinder"

Carol Bull
Gooseberry Patch Personal Shopper

My family loves submarine sandwiches, or grinders, as some folks call them. This is one way to get that meat-loving family to eat their veggies!

4 large whole wheat,
 reduced-fat sub buns
 or Kaiser rolls
cucumber slices
4 slices reduced-fat Swiss
 cheese
4 slices reduced-fat American
 or colby cheese
low-fat or no-fat Italian dressing

hot peppers to taste
lettuce leaves
mushroom slices
green onions, sliced
green pepper rings
olive slices
onion slices
tomato slices

Place the cheese slices on the bottoms and tops of the sub buns. Place the buns on a cookie sheet and toast in preheated 350 degree oven until cheese melts. Remove from oven and layer on all the vegetables. Top each sandwich with the Italian dressing. Cut in three pieces and serve hot. Garnish with parsley and hot pepper if desired. Makes 4 sandwiches.

Oven-Baked "Fries"

1 baking potato, skin on, cut into 1/2-inch wedges
1 t. paprika
1 t. vegetable oil
dash pepper and salt

Preheat oven to 425 degrees. Spray baking sheet with cooking spray. Brush potato wedges with oil and arrange on baking sheet. Sprinkle with paprika, salt and pepper. Bake for 15 to 20 minutes, until wedges are brown and tender. Serves 1.

Multi-Vegetable Pasta

Kathy Epperly
Wichita, KS

1/4 c. light olive oil
1 medium onion, chopped
1 clove garlic, minced
1/2 c. fresh parsley,
    chopped
5 c. raw vegetables,
    chopped into 3/4"
    pieces*

1 c. tomato sauce
1/4 t. black pepper
1/2 t. dried basil leaves
1/2 t. dried oregano leaves
12 oz. tubular cooked pasta,
    like rigatoni or ziti
2 T. olive oil (optional)
parmesan cheese, grated

Heat olive oil in a heavy saucepan over medium heat. Add onion, garlic and parsley. Cook and stir for 2 minutes. Add denser vegetables first and cook over medium-high heat, stirring constantly for 3 to 4 minutes. Add remaining vegetables and tomato sauce and cook, stirring for 3 to 4 more minutes. Add pepper, basil and oregano. Toss with cooked pasta, olive oil and parmesan cheese.

*Tasty vegetable combinations:
• frozen peas, carrots, red bell pepper, green onions, celery
• onions, cauliflower, peas, carrots, zucchini, green pepper
• carrots, zucchini, radishes, asparagus, cucumber, onion
• peas, red bell pepper, carrots, celery, green onions
• broccoli, cauliflower, carrots, frozen peas, olives
• red and green peppers, corn, tomatoes, celery
• asparagus, carrots, celery, mushrooms

Other easy add-ins:

julienne turkey breast (thin strips)
chopped cooked chicken
flaked canned salmon
flaked canned tuna
Swiss cheese

Vegetable Lasagna

Lisa Sett
Thousand Oaks, CA

10 oz. pkg. frozen spinach, chopped and thawed*
15 oz. container non-fat ricotta cheese
1 c. zucchini, sliced 1/4" thick
3 to 4 carrots, sliced 1/4" thick
1 c. broccoli, cut into small pieces
1 c. yellow or pan squash, sliced 1/4" thick
8 oz. pkg. lasagna noodles
26 oz. jar marinara sauce or homemade spaghetti sauce
12 oz. mozzarella cheese, sliced or grated
1/2 c. parmesan cheese, grated

Drain spinach and mix with ricotta cheese. Fill large pot with water, bring to a boil. Add vegetables and noodles to water. Cook until tender 5 to 7 minutes. Drain. Place 1/3 of sauce in a 13"x9" pan, then a layer of noodles, half the ricotta, vegetables and parmesan cheese, and a third of the mozzarella. Continue to layer with remaining ingredients, topping with sauce and mozzarella. Bake for 30 minutes at 350 degrees. If frozen, bake 1 hour.

*(or 1 cup fresh spinach, steamed and chopped)

Bruschetta

Here's a taste-tempting treat that's fun, low-calorie and easy to make!

2 red, ripe tomatoes, chopped
1/2 c. red onion, finely chopped
1/2 c. fresh basil, chopped   1/2 cucumber, chopped
1 t. red wine vinegar   8 crusty bread slices
2 t. olive oil   1 garlic clove

Combine tomatoes, onion, basil, cucumber and vinegar. Set aside for about an hour allowing the flavors to blend and the tomatoes to release their juices. Brush 8 slices of crusty bread (or English muffin halves) with olive oil. Over a medium hot fire, grill both sides of bread. Remove bread from the grill, rub with open end of a halved garlic clove and layer on the tomato mixture. Don't forget to allow the juices to soak into the bread. Delicious!

Vegetable Casserole

Marion Pfeifer
Smyrna, DE

Great flavor! My husband's favorite summer dish! Add corn on the cob and you have a meal.

3 onions, sliced
3 T. olive oil
4 medium potatoes,
   thinly sliced
2 medium zucchinis,
   thickly sliced
1 small eggplant, sliced thin

salt and pepper to taste
2 green peppers, sliced
1 T. olive oil
1 t. basil
1/2 t. garlic, minced
3 large tomatoes, peeled
   and sliced

In heavy casserole pan, sauté two of the onions in the oil until tender. Add the potatoes and cook until lightly browned. Add the zucchini and eggplant in two layers. Season with salt and pepper. Make a remaining layer of onion slices and layers of green pepper. Drizzle the tablespoon of olive oil over all and sprinkle with basil and garlic. Top with tomatoes and season again. Cover, bring to a boil and simmer gently about 25 minutes or until vegetables are tender. Serve hot, spooning down to the bottom to catch all layers. Serves 6.

Light Fettuccine Alfredo

Janice Ertola
Martinez, CA

8 oz. fettuccine, uncooked
1 T. margarine
2 garlic cloves, minced
1 c. evaporated skim milk
3 T. parmesan cheese, grated

1 T. dried basil leaves
1/8 t. nutmeg
2 T. parsley flakes
dash of pepper

Cook fettuccine to desired doneness as directed on package. Drain; return to pan. Add margarine and garlic; toss to coat. Stir in milk, cheese, basil and nutmeg; blend well. Cook over medium high heat just until thickened, about 5 minutes, stirring constantly. Sprinkle with parsley and pepper. Serves 6.

Uncooked Tomato Sauce and Pasta
Kathy Epperly
Wichita, KS

This recipe is delicious and easy.

1 lb. fresh tomatoes, chopped
2 t. mild olive oil
1 T. onion, chopped
1 clove garlic, minced
1/4 t. black pepper
1 t. dried basil leaves
12 oz. cooked pasta

1/2 c. mozzarella cheese, shredded
1/2 c. parmesan cheese, grated
small red onion, chopped
black olives, chopped

Place tomatoes, olive oil, onion, garlic, black pepper and basil in a food processor or blender and puree for 1 to 2 minutes until blended. Serve at once over 12 ounces of hot pasta that has been cooked and tossed with the mozzarella cheese and parmesan cheese. Garnish with raw red onion and chopped black olives. Serves 4.

Garden Pesto Sauce

Make your own pesto sauce to freeze for quick and easy meals!

1 T. pine nuts
2 cloves garlic
4 T. fresh basil, chopped
6 T. olive oil (try different varieties)

Blend ingredients until smooth; slowly add oil. Season as desired. Serve over pasta with freshly grated Parmesan or Asiago cheese.

Sonya's Stuffed Peppers

Sonya Collett
Yankton, SD

Here is my favorite, easy, low-fat recipe. It is one that I've adapted over my four-year married life. Hope you enjoy it as much as my husband does! This is an especially good recipe when you have tons of green peppers in the garden to use. Serve with a big, fresh salad and non-fat yogurt bars for dessert.

8 green peppers
salt
1 lb. extra lean ground beef or ground turkey
1/3 c. onion, chopped
1 1/2 c. croutons
1 c. low-fat mild cheddar cheese, shredded
2 tomatoes, chopped
1/2 t. Worcestershire sauce

Preheat oven to 350 degrees. Cut tops off of peppers and remove seeds. Precook in boiling water for 5 minutes. Sprinkle insides with salt. Brown beef or turkey with onion and drain very well. Stir in croutons, 1/2 cup cheese, tomatoes, and Worcestershire sauce. Fill peppers with mixture. Place in a shallow baking dish and cover. Bake at 350 degrees for 25 minutes. Sprinkle with remaining cheese and bake, uncovered, for 5 to 10 minutes more. Yummy!

Pull-Apart Pizza

Elizabeth VanEtten
Warwick, NY

Use low-fat cheese and you have a healthy, easy dinner.

2-10 oz. cans refrigerator
  biscuits
2 T. olive oil
1 can plum tomatoes,
  drained and chopped
small broccoli florets
  (optional)

1 c. each red and green
  pepper, chopped
1 medium onion, chopped
2 T. Italian seasonings
1/2 t. garlic powder
1/2 c. mozzarella
  cheese, shredded

Preheat oven to 400 degrees. Put the biscuits on a pizza stone or a cookie sheet. Arrange next to each other, pressing together. Brush the top of the biscuits with olive oil. Top with the vegetables and the seasoning. Sprinkle with cheese and place in the oven for 12 to 15 minutes. (Maybe a bit longer, depending on your oven.) Put it in the center of your table on hot pads; give everyone a plate and just pull off pieces. The kids really love this...just make sure to watch they don't burn themselves on the pan!

Grilled Pizza

Grilled pizza in the summertime is so easy and you have a bounty of fresh vegetable toppings to choose from.

Get all your ingredients ready...
bell peppers (red, yellow and orange) and caramelized onions (onions sautéed in olive oil until they're golden brown) are wonderful because the flavors blend together creating a real taste treat! Or, choose your toppings. Lightly oil a cookie sheet with olive oil. Using homemade dough or commercial pizza dough, spread into pizza shape on a corn-dusted surface. Transfer to cookie sheet. Cook over medium heat...if too hot, pizza will burn; if too cool, it will just puff up and remain doughy. Grill should be about 4-5 inches above the coals. Now, you're ready to slide the shell onto the grill, for only 1 or 2 minutes (watching closely so it doesn't burn). Slide it back onto the cookie sheet, grilled side up. Add the toppings, turn the temperature on the grill (if gas) down and slide the shell back onto the grill. Bake about 4-5 minutes, constantly checking bottom, so pizza doesn't burn. Yummy!

Polynesian Pork Chops

Heather Hood
Bloomington, MN

This was one of the most requested dishes when my father was cooking. Great for entertaining too!

4 center cut pork chops, cut
   1" thick
1/2 c. soy sauce
1/4 c. water
2 t. brown sugar, or brown
   sugar substitute

2 T. dehydrated bell
   pepper flakes
2 t. dehydrated minced
   onion flakes
1 clove garlic, minced
1/4 t. ground ginger

Trim excess fat from pork. Combine all ingredients except pork in shallow dish. Place pork chops in marinade. Cover; marinate in refrigerator for 3 hours or overnight, turning occasionally. Place pork chops on rack in broiler pan. Broil about 4" from heat for 10 to 13 minutes or until done. This amount of marinade is adequate for 4 pork chops.

Basic Pita Sandwiches

Kathy Epperly
Wichita, KS

1 large whole wheat pita pocket, toasted

Stuff pita pocket with one of the following combinations:

- flaked canned red salmon, ripe olives, diced avocado, orange sections
- cooked turkey breast, chopped fresh spinach, seeded tangerine chunks
- tiny cooked shrimp, diced celery, diced green bell pepper, chopped onion, pineapple chunks, Romaine lettuce
- tuna fish, chopped green onion, chopped tomatoes, chopped cucumber, chopped green bell pepper, sliced radishes, watercress

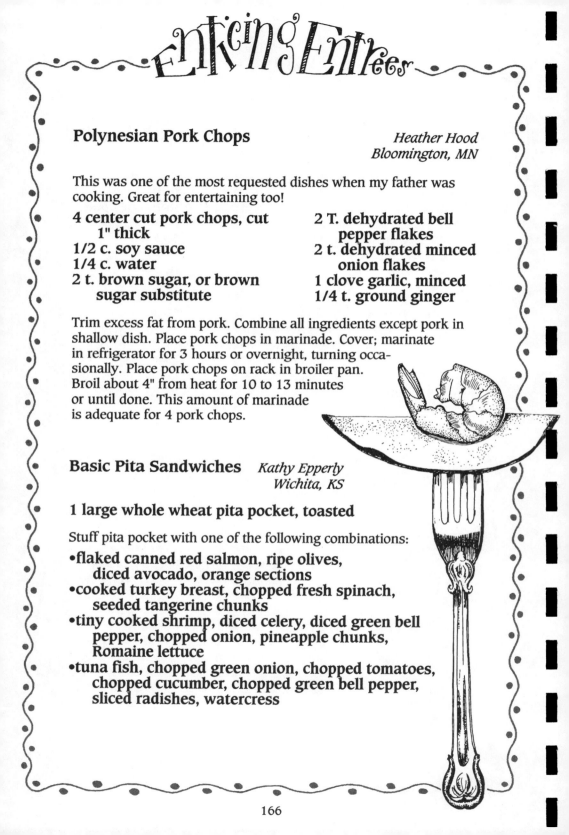

Dilled Tuna-Apple French Twists

Kathy Epperly
Wichita, KS

6 T. reduced-calorie mayonnaise
1 clove garlic, minced
1 t. dried dill weed
6.5 oz. can tuna, drained
1 large apple, cored and chopped
1/2 c. celery, chopped

1/2 c. green onion, chopped
4 French rolls
4 large romaine lettuce leaves

Combine mayonnaise, garlic and dill weed in a medium bowl. Stir in tuna, apple, celery and green onion. Halve the whole grain French rolls and top with the romaine lettuce leaves. Top with tuna apple salad and remaining roll halves. Serves 4.

Mediterranean Baked Fish

Theresa M. Nobuyuki
Laguna Hills, CA

3 1/2 lbs. whole fish, such
    as red snapper or striped
    bass, cleaned
juice of 1 lemon
salt and black pepper
3 bay leaves
6 T. olive oil
1 medium onion, sliced
2 cloves garlic, chopped

2/3 c. dry white wine
1 T. white wine vinegar
8 oz. tomatoes, chopped
2 T. tomato paste
5 T. Italian parsley, chopped
8 T. dry white bread crumbs
3 oz. feta cheese, crumbled
12 black olives or fresh
    mint to garnish

Wash the fish, pat dry. Sprinkle it inside with lemon juice and season
with salt and pepper. Tuck the bay leaves inside. Heat the oil in a pan
and cook the onion over medium heat until it is transparent. Cook
the garlic for one minute, then add the wine, wine vinegar, chopped
tomatoes, tomato paste and parsley. Season with salt and pepper. Stir
well and bring to a boil. Pour half the sauce into a shallow baking
dish (a cast iron skillet is traditional) and place the fish on top. Pour
on the remaining sauce and scatter over the bread crumbs. Bake the
fish, uncovered, in a preheated oven
at 375 degrees for 35 to 40 minutes,
until it is firm. Sprinkle over the
crumbled cheese, garnish with the
olives and serve.
Note: Black olives are high in fat;
you may want to use mint sprigs
to garnish. Serves 6.

Eat s l o w l y...
you'll actually consume less!

Catch of the Day in Foil

Judy Hand
Centre Hall, PA

Get creative with this recipe! Use celery, tomatoes, any combination of veggies that go well with fish. This is also one of those wonderful opportunities to experiment with herbs. Add small amounts of marjoram, basil, or garlic.

2 haddock, flounder, sole, or any white fish fillets (approx. 4 to 5-ozs. each)
2 small green onion, finely chopped
4 mushrooms, sliced thinly
1 c. zucchini, thinly sliced
Pepper to taste

2 t. fresh chives, minced
4 t. lemon juice
1/4 t. paprika
1 c. peeled carrots, thinly sliced
1/2 t. dill weed

Preheat oven to 450 degrees. Cut two sheets of aluminum foil large enough to enclose each fillet. Place a fillet in the center of each sheet, top each with half of the above ingredients. Fold the foil over each fillet, sealing edges very tightly. Place each package on a cookie sheet and bake for 15 to 20 minutes, or until fish flakes easily and veggies are tender to the fork. Serve each guest a fillet wrapped in their own silver pouch. Be careful as you unfold the foil, so you are not burned by the escaping steam. Serves 2.

For a light and summery meal, serve poached fish-- either hot or cold! Simply place your favorite fish in a simmering pan, and cover with fresh herbs, sliced onion, salt and a few bay leaves. Cover with a little white wine (optional) and water. Simmer uncovered until the fish flakes easily. Serve with a cold rice salad and sliced tomatoes for a wonderful and light meal. Your guests will think you've been working all day!

169

Grilled and Chilled Chicken-Rice Salad

Barbara Bargdill
Gooseberry Patch Personal Shopper

4 chicken breast halves,
   boned and skinned
1 T. soy sauce
1/2 t. lemon-pepper seasoning
1 c. red delicious apple, chopped
2 t. lemon juice
3/4 c. celery, sliced
1/3 c. raisins
2 1/2 c. long grain rice, cooked

1/4 c. plus 2 T. non-fat
   mayonnaise
1/4 c. plain non-fat
   yogurt
1/4 c. unsweetened
   apple juice
lettuce leaves
1/4 c. green onions,
   thinly sliced

Brush chicken breast with soy sauce and sprinkle with lemon-pepper seasoning. Coat grill rack with vegetable cooking spray, and place on grill over medium hot coals. Place chicken breast on rack, and cook 5 to 6 minutes on each side, or until chicken is tender. Remove chicken from grill, and let it cool slightly. Cut chicken into one-inch pieces. Combine chopped apple and lemon juice in a large bowl. Add chicken, sliced celery, raisins, and cooked rice to apple mixture; toss well. Combine mayonnaise, yogurt, and apple juice in a small bowl; stir well. Pour mayonnaise mixture over chicken mixture, and toss gently to combine. Cover and chill thoroughly. Just before serving, spoon mixture into lettuce-lined bowl. Sprinkle with green onions. Yield: 6 servings.

Skin-on Mashed Potatoes

2 to 3 medum white or baking potatoes
1/4 c. skim milk
butter to taste
garlic salt
pepper

Scrub potatoes, cut into quarters (do not peel) and boil for twenty to twenty-five minutes in medium saucepan of salted water. When soft, drain and mash. After potatoes are as fluffy as possible, add milk a little at a time, continuing to stir with fork. Add seasonings to taste. The skins add vitamins and wonderful flavor; you won't need much butter! Serves 2.

De~
Liteful
Salads, Soups
& Sides

Soup's On

Grilled Vegetable Salad

Barbara Bargdill
Gooseberry Patch Personal Shopper

1/3 c. white balsamic vinegar	1/4 t. salt
2 T. olive oil	1/4 t. pepper
2 shallots, finely chopped	1 1/2 t. molasses
1 t. dried Italian seasoning	

Vegetables:

1/2 lb. carrots, scraped	2 yellow squash
1 sweet red pepper	1 large onion
1 sweet yellow pepper	2 zucchini

Combine first seven ingredients in bowl. Set aside. Cut vegetables into large pieces and add to vinegar mixture, tossing to coat. Let stand 30 minutes, stirring occasionally. Drain, reserve vinegar mixture. Arrange in a grill basket that has been coated with cooking spray. Cook, covered with grill lid over medium to hot coals, 15 to 20 minutes, turning occasionally. Return vegetables to reserved vinegar mixture, tossing gently. Cover and refrigerate overnight. Yields 6 cups.

Green Salad with Beef and Fruit

Kathy Epperly
Wichita, KS

4 c. Romaine leaves, torn	2 c. lean roast beef strips
3 c. spinach, torn	1/2 c. olive oil
1 1/2 c. nectarines, sliced	3 T. red wine vinegar
1 avocado, sliced	1 T. fresh horseradish,
12 cherry tomatoes, halved	chopped

Combine Romaine leaves, spinach, nectarines, avocado, tomatoes and roast beef. Mix together in a small bowl the olive oil, red wine vinegar and horseradish until combined. Pour over the salad and toss to coat. Serves 4.

Rainbow Rotini Pasta Salad

Lisa DelPrete
Rockland, MA

For those of you who enjoy the taste of garlic, I usually put a couple of cloves of garlic in the dressing and let sit for an hour or so. Then remove the cloves and pour over the salad.

1 or 2 boxes of tri-colored rotini pasta
red/green/yellow peppers (use a variety for color)
onions (yellow, or use Bermuda onions for color)
cheese (your favorite kinds, chunked or shredded)

tomatoes
carrots
cucumbers
broccoli
Italian dressing

Cook pasta, drain and let cool. The amount of vegetables you use depends on your taste. (Use lots of your favorites...or whatever is fresh and in season.) Add cut-up vegetables to the pasta. Mix Italian dressing to the above and stir until evenly coated. One large bottle is usually enough depending on your taste. For best results let pasta sit overnight, and add more dressing if needed before serving.

*Try new pasta salads as
"light" main meals. Finish with tastes of
special cheeses and breads and complement
with your favorite glass of wine or sparkling water.
Relax and enjoy--who needs to
rush and clean up?*

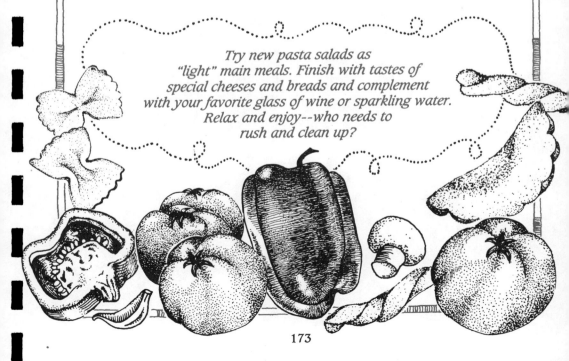

Kiwi Salad

Kathy Epperly
Wichita, KS

2 c. pineapple chunks,
  canned or fresh
6 kiwis, peeled and sliced
1 c. walnuts, chopped

1 c. red grapes, seedless
3 bananas, sliced
2 naval oranges

Toss salad ingredients together.

Sauce:

1 1/2 T. lemon peel, grated
1 t. fresh ginger root, grated
2 T. honey
1 T. lemon juice

3/4 c. non-fat plain
  yogurt
3/4 c. reduced-calorie
  mayonnaise

Combine fruit ingredients
and serve the sauce
in a pretty cruet
on the side.

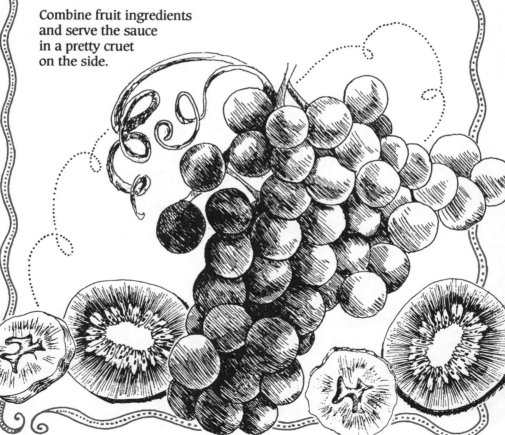

Spinach Fruit Salad

Kathy Epperly
Wichita, KS

This salad gets 4 stars!

3 c. whole strawberries, hulled
3 c. Romaine lettuce, torn
3 c. stemmed watercress
   (if available)
2 naval oranges, peeled,
   sectioned and chopped
1/4 c. almonds, toasted

3 c. spinach leaves, torn
1/2 c. celery, chopped
1/2 c. green bell pepper,
   chopped
1 grapefruit, peeled,
   sectioned and
   chopped

Combine salad mixture ingredients.

Sauce:

1/2 c. strawberries, hulled
   and sliced
1 t. honey

2 T. red wine vinegar
2 T. orange juice

Puree sauce ingredients in a food processor or blender. Toss together sauce with salad.

Spinach Salad with Light Poppy Seed Dressing

Marie Alana Gardner
North Tonawanda, NY

2 c. packed spinach leaves,
   stems removed, torn into
   bite-size pieces
1 Granny Smith apple, cubed

1 navel orange, peeled
   and sectioned or
   cubed
1/4 c. red onion,
   chopped

Combine salad ingredients with dressing, toss well and serve.

Dressing:

1/3 c. light mayonnaise
1/3 c. plain non-fat yogurt
2 t. sugar

2 t. vinegar
1 t. poppy seeds

Mix mayonnaise and yogurt together until blended. Stir in sugar, vinegar and poppy seeds.

Romaine-Orange Salad

Kathy Epperly
Wichita, KS

8 c. Romaine lettuce, torn
2 c. chicory, torn
1/3 c. walnuts, chopped

2 naval oranges peeled,
    sectioned and sliced
4 green onions, sliced

Combine salad ingredients in a large bowl.

Sauce:

2 T. white wine vinegar
1 t. lemon juice
2 t. dijon mustard

1/8 t. pepper
1/2 c. olive oil

Mix together sauce ingredients and pour over salad. Toss to coat.
Serves 6.

Basil-Tomato Salad

Barbara Truax
St. Louis, MO

5 large tomatoes, cut into slices
1 lb. low-fat mozzarella cheese,
    thinly sliced
4 to 6 T. olive oil
1/3 c. fresh basil
    leaves, chopped

salt and pepper
    to taste

Alternate layers of cheese and
tomatoes on a platter
and drizzle with oil,
basil, salt and
pepper.

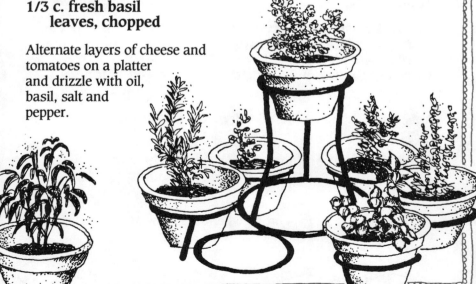

Super Rice Salad

Margaret Riley
Tonawanda, NY

2 c. rice or orzo (rice-shaped
    pasta), cooked
1 can corn niblets, drained
1 c. frozen baby peas
1/4 c. red onion, chopped
1/2 c. green pepper, diced

1/2 c. pimiento olives
    sliced
1/2 c. celery, diced
1/2 c. red pepper, diced
8 T. Italian dressing

Combine all ingredients except salad dressing in a large bowl and toss gently. Add salad dressing and toss again. Cover and refrigerate until ready to use.

Pea Salad

Judy Borecky
Escondido, CA

2- 16 oz. cans black-eyed peas, drained
    or 4 c. cooked
1/2 green pepper, chopped
1/4 c. red onion, chopped
1/2 recipe "Best Ever" salad dressing

Mix and marinate overnight in refrigerator.

"Best-Ever" Salad Dressing:

1/2 c. balsamic or rice vinegar
1/4 c. olive oil or lemon juice
    or use a mixture
1/2 c. water
1 packet Italian salad dressing

Whisk well.

Share magazines, catalogs and
paperbacks with your senior center,
nursing home or hospital.

Mexican Salad

Cheryl Parker
Portland, OR

The more this sits, the more the flavors blend together.

15 oz. can corn
15 oz. can black beans
10 oz. jar salsa

5 stalks celery, chopped
cilantro to taste

Drain corn and black beans; mix together. Add salsa, celery and cilantro. Serves 6.

Dutch Chicken Salad

Vicky Perkins
Central Lake, MI

A low-fat treat for those hot-night summertime suppers.

2 c. spiral pasta, uncooked
1 chicken breast, poached
1 yellow delicious apple
1 Granny Smith apple
20 oz. can pineapple tidbits

1/2 round gouda
cheese
1/2 c. almonds, sliced
1 T. poppy seeds

Dressing:

2/3 c. non-fat sour cream
1/3 c. non-fat, non-cholesterol mayonnaise

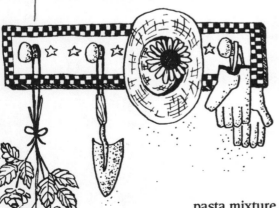

Cook, drain and cool pasta. Poach chicken in microwave with water to cover, about 8 minutes on high. Remove from liquid, cool and dice. Core and chop apples; do not peel. Drain pineapple. Peel wax from cheese; dice. Mix all ingredients except poppy seeds with cooled pasta in a large bowl. Make dressing and mix well with pasta mixture. Stir in poppy seeds until well blended. Refrigerate before serving. Serves 4 to 6.

Grilled Chicken Garden Salad

Deb Weiser
Gooseberry Patch Warehouse

Especially delicious in the summer. Garnish with homemade star and heart croutons!

4 boneless, skinless chicken breasts
fat-free Italian dressing
4 slices of bread or one small French bread loaf
seasoned salt or butter-flavored sprinkles
1 head lettuce, leaf or romaine, torn
1 medium red onion, sliced and ringed

2 carrots, sliced or shredded
1 medium red or green pepper, sliced
2 tomatoes, chunked
12 oz. low-fat parmesan cheese or mozzarella cheese

Marinate chicken in Italian dressing for one hour in fridge. Grill chicken in dressing until well done. When done, cut into strips or chunks. Cube bread, or use mini cookie cutters (stars, hearts) to cut bread. Toast on griddle with no-stick spray or butter. Sprinkle with seasonings or butter sprinkles. Keep turning. Prepare 4 plates with lettuce on each. Arrange onions, carrots, peppers and tomatoes on lettuce. Sprinkle with cheese and Italian dressing. Place chicken and homemade croutons on top. Eat while chicken is hot or cold.

Chicken Chili Salad

Kathy Epperly
Wichita, KS

2 c. chicken breast strips, cooked
2 medium tomatoes, chopped
1 c. carrot, shredded

1 c. celery, chopped
6 c. Romaine lettuce leaves, torn
3 T. green onion, chopped

Combine salad ingredients.

Sauce:

2 c. non-fat cheddar cheese, shredded
2/3 c. low fat milk

3 T. mild chili peppers, chopped
3 T. ripe olives, chopped

Place cheese and milk in a saucepan over medium heat. Stir until cheese has melted and mixture is smooth. Add chili peppers and ripe olives. Pour over salad and toss. Serves 4.

Potato Salad

Marlene Wetzel-Dellagatta
Egg Harbor City, NJ

10 medium red potatoes, unpeeled (about 3 lbs.)
1 1/2 T. olive oil
2 leeks, coarsely chopped
3/4 c. green onions, sliced
1/2 c. parsley, chopped
1/4 c. pimiento, diced

1/2 c. plain low-fat yogurt
3 T. white wine vinegar
1 T. Dijon mustard
1/2 t. salt
1/2 t. pepper
1/4 t. dried, whole tarragon

Put potatoes in Dutch oven, cover with water. Bring to boil, then reduce heat and simmer for 25 minutes or until tender. Drain and cool. Sauté leeks for 5 minutes until brown. Cut potatoes into 1/4" slices. Combine potato slices, leeks, green onions, parsley and pimiento. Set aside. In another bowl, combine yogurt and next 5 ingredients. Stir, then add to potato mixture. Toss to coat. Cover and chill. Yields 8 servings, 1 cup each.

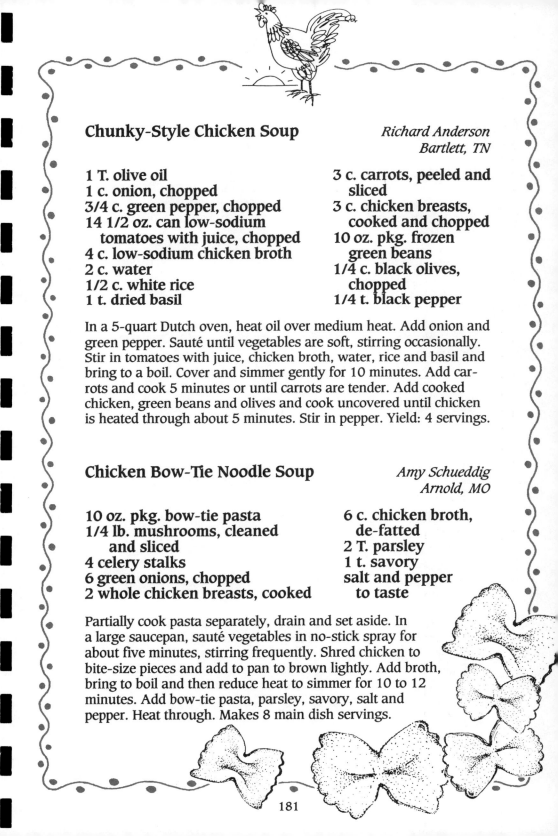

Chunky-Style Chicken Soup

Richard Anderson
Bartlett, TN

1 T. olive oil
1 c. onion, chopped
3/4 c. green pepper, chopped
14 1/2 oz. can low-sodium
  tomatoes with juice, chopped
4 c. low-sodium chicken broth
2 c. water
1/2 c. white rice
1 t. dried basil

3 c. carrots, peeled and
  sliced
3 c. chicken breasts,
  cooked and chopped
10 oz. pkg. frozen
  green beans
1/4 c. black olives,
  chopped
1/4 t. black pepper

In a 5-quart Dutch oven, heat oil over medium heat. Add onion and green pepper. Sauté until vegetables are soft, stirring occasionally. Stir in tomatoes with juice, chicken broth, water, rice and basil and bring to a boil. Cover and simmer gently for 10 minutes. Add carrots and cook 5 minutes or until carrots are tender. Add cooked chicken, green beans and olives and cook uncovered until chicken is heated through about 5 minutes. Stir in pepper. Yield: 4 servings.

Chicken Bow-Tie Noodle Soup

Amy Schueddig
Arnold, MO

10 oz. pkg. bow-tie pasta
1/4 lb. mushrooms, cleaned
  and sliced
4 celery stalks
6 green onions, chopped
2 whole chicken breasts, cooked

6 c. chicken broth,
  de-fatted
2 T. parsley
1 t. savory
salt and pepper
  to taste

Partially cook pasta separately, drain and set aside. In a large saucepan, sauté vegetables in no-stick spray for about five minutes, stirring frequently. Shred chicken to bite-size pieces and add to pan to brown lightly. Add broth, bring to boil and then reduce heat to simmer for 10 to 12 minutes. Add bow-tie pasta, parsley, savory, salt and pepper. Heat through. Makes 8 main dish servings.

Meatball Soup

Shirll Kosmal
Gooseberry Patch Warehouse

1/2 lb. lean ground beef
1 envelope zesty Italian
    salad dressing mix
1/4 c. plain bread crumbs
6 c. water

8 oz. can stewed tomatoes
4 stalks celery, chopped
1 carrot, chopped
1 1/2 c. instant brown rice

Mix meat, 1 teaspoon of salad dressing mix and bread crumbs in small bowl. Shape into 1-inch meatballs; set aside. Bring water to boil in large saucepan. Add meatballs, remaining salad dressing mix and vegetables. Bring to boil. Stir in rice. Return to boil. cover, reduce heat and simmer 5 minutes. Remove from heat and let stand 5 minutes. Makes 10 servings and has only 140 calories with 5 grams of fat.

Irish Potato Soup

Candy Hannigan
Monument, CO

We love homemade soup at our house, and potato is one of our favorites. This is a Christmas Eve tradition at the Hannigans'. I used to thicken the soup with margarine and flour and whole milk, but now I do it with a lot less fat and just as much flavor.

5 c. redskin potatoes,
    peeled, cubed
2 cans chicken broth*
1 c. water
1/2 c. evaporated skim milk
1/2 t. pepper

1 t. salt
6 oz. turkey ham, chopped
1/3 c. instant mashed
    potatoes
1/2 T. fresh parsley,
    snipped

Peel potatoes and cube. Place in large pot with chicken broth and water. Cover and simmer until fork tender, about 30 minutes. Add evaporated skim milk, pepper, salt and turkey ham. Heat on low until hot. Stir in instant mashed potatoes to thicken. (We like ours thick, so you may adjust with more or less milk). Garnish with lots of snipped parsley. Can be topped with shredded Swiss cheese.

*Refrigerate 30 minutes and you can remove the fat from the top.

Tomato Soup

Margaret Towne
San Jose, CA

Use sweet, fresh summer tomatoes. Freeze some to enjoy the taste of summer during those long winter months.

2 1/2 lbs. fresh, ripe tomatoes   **1 green pepper, chopped**
2 carrots, sliced   **3 whole cloves**
3 stalks celery, chopped   **2 T. lemon juice**
1 onion, chopped   **salt and pepper to taste**

Coarsely chop the tomatoes and put them in a soup pot with 1 cup water. Add carrots, celery, onion, green pepper and cloves. Bring to a boil, reduce heat and simmer for 20 minutes. Strain. Add lemon juice and salt and pepper to taste. Makes 4 cups.

Mixed Vegetable Stew

Nancy Campbell
Bellingham, WA

Serve hot with a crunchy loaf of bread. This recipe is a family favorite with fresh vegetables from the garden. In the winter I use our own canned tomatoes. Delicious!

2 onions, chopped
1 green pepper, chopped
2 large tomatoes,
   peeled and chopped
3 small zucchini squash, sliced
   in 1/4" slices
3 small yellow crooked neck
   squash, sliced in 1/4" slices
1 t. hot pepper sauce
2 T. butter
1 clove garlic, minced

1/2 t. curry powder
1 t. chili powder
salt and pepper to taste
1 medium eggplant,
   chopped into bite-
   size pieces
Optional: Mozzarella
   cheese, shredded
   (sprinkle on top of
   stew just before
   serving)

Put above ingredients in large kettle. Cover and simmer on low 1 hour, stirring frequently. Serves 6. Note: Do not add any liquid. Veggies make their own juice.

Walk through your garden early in the morning, when the dew is still light, and enjoy the sights and sounds... wonderful gratification after all your hard work!

Black Bean Soup

Amy Schueddig
Arnold, MO

1 c. dried black beans,
   sorted and rinsed
5 1/2 c. chicken broth, de-fatted
1/3 c. red wine
1 c. onions, chopped
4 cloves garlic, minced
3 carrots, coarsely chopped
5 stalks celery, coarsely chopped
1 bay leaf
1 T. snipped fresh parsley
1 to 1 1/4 t. ground cumin

1/2 t. ground black
   pepper
1 t. red pepper
1/4 t. liquid smoke
2 hard-cooked egg
   whites (discard yolks)
1/2 c. (2 oz.) reduced-
   fat Monterey Jack
   cheese, shredded

In a large saucepan, combine beans and broth. Bring to boil, then reduce the heat. Cover and simmer for 30 to 40 minutes or until the beans are fork-tender. Meanwhile in a large skillet, combine wine, onions and garlic. Cook and stir until the onions are tender. Add the onion mixture to the beans. Then add the carrots, celery, bay leaf, parsley, cumin, black pepper, red pepper, and liquid smoke. Bring to boil, then reduce the heat. Cover and simmer for 20 to 30 minutes or until the vegetables are tender. Remove and discard the bay leaf.

Transfer one-fourth of the mixture to a blender. Blend until smooth. Return the mixture to the saucepan with the remaining bean mixture. Heat through. Ladle the soup into individual bowls. Top with chopped egg whites and cheese. Makes 4 main dish servings.

Oven Fries

Janice Ertola
Martinez, CA

My family loves these more than fat-filled French fries. We dip them in catsup.

3 potatoes   **garlic powder**

Preheat oven to 425 degrees. Spray a cookie sheet with non-stick spray. Slice potatoes very thin (about 1/8" thick). Spread on cookie sheet and sprinkle with garlic powder. Bake at 425 degrees for 10 to 15 minutes, turn and bake an additional 10 minutes. Potatoes should be light brown and crisp. Serves 4.

Potato Skins

Amy Schueddig
Arnold, MO

12 medium baking potatoes
1 c. (4 oz.) reduced-fat Monterey Jack cheese, finely shredded
1/3 c. fresh chives, snipped

1 c. (4 oz.) reduced-fat cheddar cheese, finely shredded

Preheat the oven to 425 degrees. Using a fork, prick the potatoes. Bake for 40 to 50 minutes or until tender. Cut the potatoes lengthwise into quarters. Scoop out the pulp with a small spoon, leaving 1/4"-thick shells. (Set aside the pulp for another use.) Spray a cookie sheet with no-stick spray. Place the potato shells on the sheet with the skin sides down. Spray the potatoes with the no-stick spray. Bake at 425 degrees for 10 to 15 minutes or until crisp. Sprinkle the Monterey Jack cheese and cheddar cheese on the potatoes, then bake about 2 minutes more or until the cheeses are melted. Sprinkle with chives and serve warm. Makes 48 potato skins.

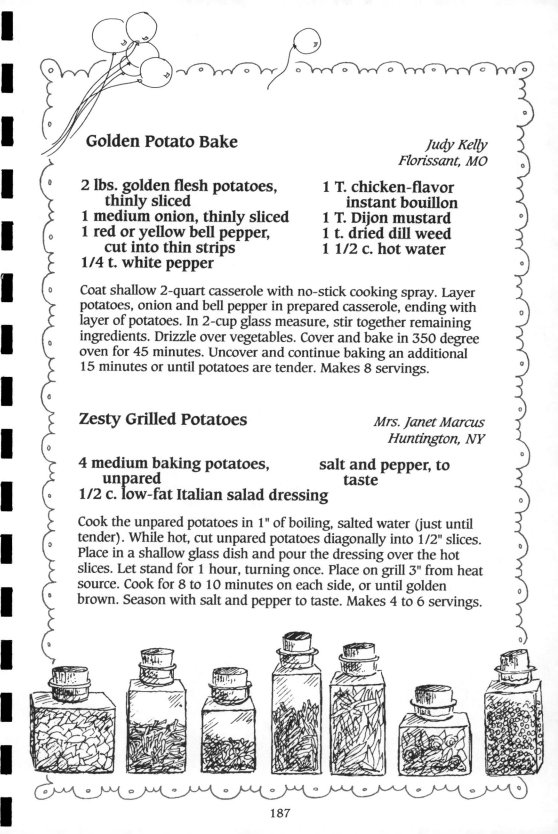

Golden Potato Bake

Judy Kelly
Florissant, MO

2 lbs. golden flesh potatoes,
    thinly sliced
1 medium onion, thinly sliced
1 red or yellow bell pepper,
    cut into thin strips
1/4 t. white pepper

1 T. chicken-flavor
    instant bouillon
1 T. Dijon mustard
1 t. dried dill weed
1 1/2 c. hot water

Coat shallow 2-quart casserole with no-stick cooking spray. Layer potatoes, onion and bell pepper in prepared casserole, ending with layer of potatoes. In 2-cup glass measure, stir together remaining ingredients. Drizzle over vegetables. Cover and bake in 350 degree oven for 45 minutes. Uncover and continue baking an additional 15 minutes or until potatoes are tender. Makes 8 servings.

Zesty Grilled Potatoes

Mrs. Janet Marcus
Huntington, NY

4 medium baking potatoes,
    unpared
1/2 c. low-fat Italian salad dressing

salt and pepper, to
    taste

Cook the unpared potatoes in 1" of boiling, salted water (just until tender). While hot, cut unpared potatoes diagonally into 1/2" slices. Place in a shallow glass dish and pour the dressing over the hot slices. Let stand for 1 hour, turning once. Place on grill 3" from heat source. Cook for 8 to 10 minutes on each side, or until golden brown. Season with salt and pepper to taste. Makes 4 to 6 servings.

Stuffed Mushrooms

Debbie Benjamin

1 lb. medium-sized fresh
   mushrooms
1/2 c. onion, chopped
1 T. vegetable oil

8 oz. fat-free cheddar
   cheese, shredded
2 T. parsley

Remove stems from mushrooms, chop enough stems to make 1/2 cup. Sauté stems with onion in oil until tender. Combine cheese, parsley and mushroom mixture in food processor or blender. Process until finely chopped and blended. Fill each mushroom cap with a heaping amount of mixture. Bake at 350 degrees for 15 minutes. Serves 8.

Cheesy Italian Green Beans

*Mary K. Murray
Mount Vernon, OH*

Green beans topped with fresh tomato slices and mozzarella cheese...a great side dish!

1 envelope instant
   onion soup mix
1/2 c. boiling water
9 oz. pkg. frozen Italian
   green beans
3 tomatoes, sliced
   and peeled

1 t. dried onion,
   minced
1/2 t. salt
1 t. oregano
2 oz. part-skim
   mozzarella cheese,
   shredded

Dissolve onion soup mix in boiling water; add the green beans. Cook 3 minutes. Turn the beans and liquid into a shallow 6-cup baking dish. Top with tomato slices; sprinkle with minced onion, salt, oregano and cheese. Bake at 325 degrees for 30 minutes, or until beans are bubbly and cheese is melted and lightly browned. Yields 6 servings. (58 calories per serving)

Lemony Herbed Asparagus

Delores Berg
Selah, WA

Healthy asparagus combined with a low-calorie sauce.

1 lb. asparagus spears
1 T. olive oil or margarine
1/8 t. dried basil, crushed

1/8 t. dried oregano, crushed
dash of pepper
1 t. lemon juice

Cook asparagus in water until tender. Meanwhile, in another saucepan combine oil or margarine, basil, oregano and dash of pepper. Cook and stir, over medium heat, until heated through; remove from heat. Stir in lemon juice. Drain asparagus and transfer to serving platter. Drizzle with lemon mixture. Makes 4 servings. (58 calories per serving)

Strawberry Bread

Diane Donato
West Chicago, IL

1 1/2 c. all-purpose flour
1/2 c. granulated sugar
1/2 t. baking soda
1/2 t. cinnamon
1/4 t. salt
1 c. frozen strawberries, thawed
(reserve 1 T. of juice)

1/4 c. vegetable oil
1 large egg white,
lightly beaten
1 oz. pecans, coarsely
chopped
1/2 c. light cream
cheese

Preheat oven to 350 degrees. Spray a 9"x5" loaf pan with non-stick cooking spray. In a large bowl, combine the first five ingredients. Make a well in the center of the mixture. Pour strawberries, oil, egg white and pecans into the well and mix thoroughly. Pour batter into pan and bake for 45 to 50 minutes or until toothpick comes out clean. Cool completely on a rack. Mix the reserved juice into the cream cheese for the accompanying spread.

Homemade French Bread

Lynda Tatman
Fresno, CA

I used to make this easy French bread recipe three to four times a week. I used to grind the whole wheat berries into flour with a hand wheat grinder. The smell of the fresh ground flour was delicious all by itself. The smell of this bread would always bring the family running from outdoors. We also would skim the cream off the fresh milk and put it into a blender with cold ice water to make fresh butter. There was nothing like it when we were teenagers... you couldn't beat the taste of warm bread with the homemade butter on top. Yum!! For an extra sweet tooth treat we would put Grandma's homemade elderberry jelly on the bread. Just remembering, I can smell and taste this fresh bread. Great for making cinnamon rolls too!

2 T. yeast
2 t. honey
2 1/2 c. warm water
1 T. olive oil

4 1/2 c. unbleached flour
1/4 c. whole wheat flour
2 t. salt

Let yeast dissolve in honey and warm water. Let stand until yeast foams to the top. Add olive oil and stir. Then add flour and salt mixture and knead on floured board about 5 minutes. Divide dough in 2 parts. Make in shape of French bread loaves. Put on greased cookie sheet. Let rise 25 minutes. Make 4 slits across top of bread. Bake at 400 degrees for 25 minutes. Let cool. Brush with oil.

Health-Nut Bread

Judy Hand
Centre Hall, PA

1 c. unbleached flour
1/4 c. instant non-fat dry milk
1 pkg. dry yeast
1 T. brown sugar
1 t. salt
1t. ground cinnamon,
   cardamom or coriander
1 1/4 c. hot water
   (125 to 130 degrees)

3 T. margarine
1 T. molasses
1/4 c. wheat germ
1/4 c. walnuts or
   pecans, chopped
1/2 c. oatmeal
2 c. whole wheat flour
1/4 c. raisins

Combine the unbleached flour, dry milk, yeast, sugar, salt and cinnamon, mixing slightly. In another bowl, place hot water and quickly add margarine and molasses. Add these liquid ingredients all at once to the flour mixture and mix on low speed. When barely mixed, turn to medium speed and beat for 4 minutes. Reduce speed, add wheat germ, nuts, oatmeal, and 1 cup of the whole wheat flour. Gradually add remaining cup of flour until a smooth dough is formed. Knead dough 5 minutes, adding raisins the last 2 minutes. Place in oiled bowl and roll dough oiled side up. Cover and let rise until double in size. Punch dough down and turn out onto lightly floured board. Roll out into a 9"x5"x3" pan. Cover and let rise again until double in size. Place pan in unheated oven, turn to 375 degrees and bake 15 minutes. Cover loosely with foil, and continue baking 35 to 45 minutes. Turn loaf of bread onto rack. It will sound hollow when tapped. If not, return to the oven in pan for 5 more minutes. Cool and slice.

Whole Wheat Quick Bread

Mel Wolk
St. Peters, MO

2 c. whole wheat flour
1/2 c. soy flour
1 t. baking soda
1 t. baking powder
1/4 c. wheat germ

1/4 c. dry milk powder
1/2 t. salt
1 1/2 c. milk
1/2 c. honey or molasses

Combine dry ingredients. Add milk and honey, stirring until moistened. Let stand in greased 9"x5" loaf pan while oven is preheating to 350 degrees. Bake for 35 to 50 minutes, or until a toothpick inserted in the center comes out clean. Let cool in pan for 10 minutes, then turn out onto a cooling rack. This also freezes very well.

Cottage Cheese Rolls

Carol Sheets
Gooseberry Patch Customer Service

2 pkgs. active yeast
1/2 c. lukewarm water
2 c. cottage cheese
1/4 c. sugar

2 t. salt
1/2 t. baking soda
2 eggs
4 1/2 c. sifted flour

Sprinkle yeast on lukewarm water; stir to dissolve. Heat cottage cheese until lukewarm. Combine cottage cheese, sugar, salt, baking soda, eggs, yeast, and one cup flour in bowl. Beat with electric mixer at medium speed until smooth, about two minutes, scraping bowl occasionally. Or beat with spoon until batter is smooth. Gradually add enough flour to make a soft dough that leaves the sides of the bowl. Place dough in greased bowl; turn over to grease top. Cover and let rise in warm place until doubled in size, about one and a half hours. Turn dough onto lightly floured surface. Divide dough into 24 equal pieces. Let rise until doubled, about 45 minutes. Bake at 350 degrees for 20 minutes until golden brown. Remove from pans; cool on racks. Makes 24 rolls.

Little Extras...
Dressings, Salsas & Such

Kabob Sauce

ATLAS E-Z

Herbed Olive Oil

Salsa

Herbs for Salsa

No Salt Shake

BALL
IDEAL
PAT. JULY 1908

Raspberry Vinegar

Fat-Free Vinaigrette

Deborah Peters
Breinigsville, PA

1/2 c. flavored vinegar
2 t. Worcestershire sauce
4 t. sugar or sweetener
2 garlic cloves, crushed

1/4 t. pepper
1 T. Dijon mustard
2 T. water

Combine the ingredients in a screw-top jar or bottle and shake well.
Refrigerate.

Low-fat Creamy Dijon
Parmesan Salad Dressing

Jeannine English
Wylie, TX

Excellent over your favorite fruit salad, pasta, or plain grilled chicken.

1 c. buttermilk
8 oz. non-fat sour cream
1/3 c. parmesan cheese, grated

1 T. Dijon mustard
1 t. fresh lemon juice
1/4 t. coarse ground
     black pepper

Whirl together all the ingredients in a food processor until smooth.
Makes 1 1/2 cups. (1 gram fat per 2 tablespoons)

Low-Cal Thousand Island Dressing

Margaret Riley
Tonawanda, NY

1/2 c. light mayonnaise
1/2 c. low-fat yogurt
2 T. red pepper, chopped

2 T. pickle relish
2 T. chili sauce

Whisk in bowl. Makes 1 1/2 cups. (2 tablespoons = 30 calories,
2 grams fat)

*Scooped-out veggies make great edible
containers for salads, rice and dips.*

No-Salt Seasoning

DiAnn Voegele
Mascoutah, IL

1/2 t. garlic powder
1/4 t. thyme leaves
1/4 t. onion powder
1/4 t. paprika
1/4 t. ground black pepper

1/4 t. white pepper*
1/4 t. dried lemon peel
1/4 t. dry mustard
1/8 t. celery seed

Mix all ingredients. Store in covered container or zipper lock bag. I save empty spice bottles with shaker tops...they work great. Makes about 1/2 cup.

*I sometimes just use lemon pepper, instead of white pepper and dried lemon peel.

Raspberry Vinegar

Barbara Bargdill
Gooseberry Patch Personal Shopper

1 pound raspberries, fresh or
    frozen without sugar
4 c. red or white wine vinegar

1 c. sugar

In a non-metallic pan, simmer all ingredients slowly for 10 minutes. Refrigerate covered in a non-metallic container for 3 weeks. Strain through a mesh sieve, pressing pulp to extract juice from berries. Store in refrigerator. Use this in place of plain vinegar in your favorite low-calorie salad dressing or marinade.

Flavored Vinegar

Deborah Peters
Breinigsville, PA

white or red vinegar
2 to 3 large garlic
   cloves (optional)

enough herbs to loosely
   fill bottle

I use wine or salad dressing bottles that I have sterilized. Fill the bottle with the garlic and herbs of your choice. Fill the bottle with vinegar. Close tightly. Store in dark place for two weeks to "cure." You can opt for white vinegar or red vinegar, depending upon the choice of herbs and the flavor combination you enjoy. Trial and error seems to be the best way to decide.

Suggested herbs:

tarragon
oregano & garlic
thyme & garlic
dill & garlic
mint (any variety)
basil & garlic

Suggested fruits:

raspberries
cranberries & strawberries
blueberries & orange peel
cherries & lemon peel
vanilla bean pieces
   & citrus peel

To make fruit vinegars, I fill the bottle 1/4 to 1/3 of the way full with my choice of fruit and then fill with white vinegar.

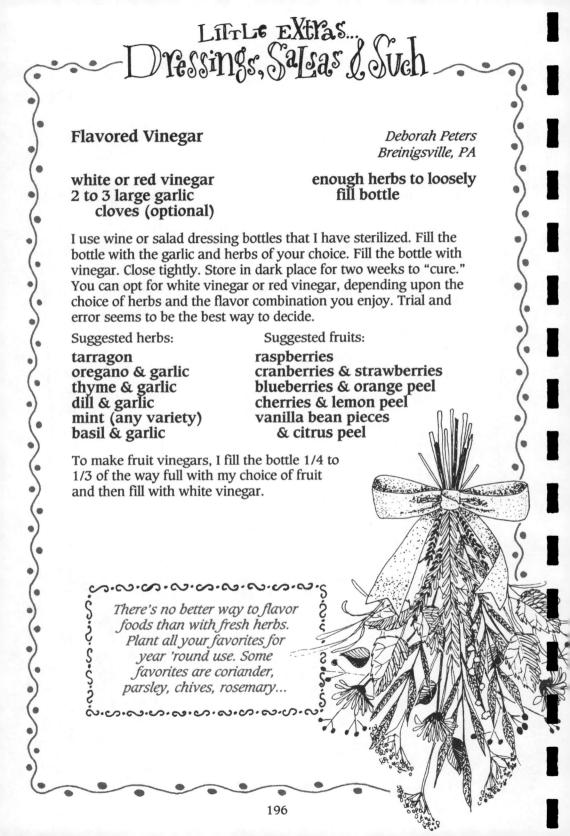

There's no better way to flavor foods than with fresh herbs. Plant all your favorites for year 'round use. Some favorites are coriander, parsley, chives, rosemary...

Skinny Mint Dip

Judy Hand
Centre Hall, PA

In order to have fresh mint all year long, I freeze washed mint leaves in plastic containers with waxed paper between each layer.

2 c. small curd low-fat
  cottage cheese
2 T. white vinegar
1 T. fresh basil or 1 t. dried basil
  (can adjust to taste)
salt and pepper to taste

1/4 c. scallions,
  chopped
3 T. fresh parsley,
  minced
1 T. fresh mint, sliced
  ribbon thin

Place cottage cheese, vinegar, basil, salt, and pepper in blender and blend until smooth. Remove mixture from blender and add mint, scallions and parsley. Chill and serve with raw, fresh vegetables.

Horseradish Sauce

Jo Baker
Litchfield, IL

3 T. horseradish, grated
1 c. low-fat mayonnaise

1 t. Dijon mustard

Combine ingredients and refrigerate until needed.

Mustard Sauce

Jo Baker
Litchfield, IL

1/2 c. non-fat cottage cheese
1/2 c. non-fat yogurt
6 T. Dijon mustard
1/4 c. fresh dill

Combine all ingredients and refrigerate until needed.

...basil, dill, garlic and thyme.

Zesty Herbal Mustard

Judy Hand
Centre Hall, PA

2 c. prepared mustard
2 T. tarragon
1 t. dill weed
1/4 c. cider vinegar

1/4 c. parsley flakes
1 t. oregano
1 t. basil, crushed

Mix all ingredients except vinegar together. Slowly stir vinegar into mixture. Refrigerate at least 3 days prior to using. Not only does this make a delicious low-calorie alternative for use on sandwiches (instead of mayonnaise), it makes a lovely hostess gift or stocking stuffer.

Barbecue Sauce

Jo Baker
Litchfield, IL

Use for marinating or basting sauce for meat.

1/2 c. low-calorie catsup

2 c. diet cola

Combine beverage and catsup until well blended. Store in airtight container in refrigerator.

Salsa

Jo Baker
Litchfield, IL

Serve with tortilla chips.

2 medium tomatoes, peeled and chopped
3 T. green chilies, diced
2 T. onion, minced
1 t. vegetable oil
1 t. vinegar
1/2 t. salt

Combine all ingredients well.
Cover and refrigerate until chilled.

Kabob Sauce

Janet C. Myers
Reading, PA

This recipe was given to me by the butcher at my local farmer's market. It's wonderful! You do not need to marinate the meat. Cooking at the gas grill, my husband just brushes the sauce frequently over kabobs, made of 1 1/2" cubes of beef and pork, alternating the meat with mushrooms and red and green peppers. Takes about 10 to 15 minutes per side.

1/2 c. soy sauce   1 t. ginger
1/2 c. orange juice   1 t. sugar
1/2 c. olive oil   one clove of garlic

Mix all ingredients together. When grilling, use heavy duty aluminum foil under kabobs and meat will stay juicy. Sauce for 8 kabobs.

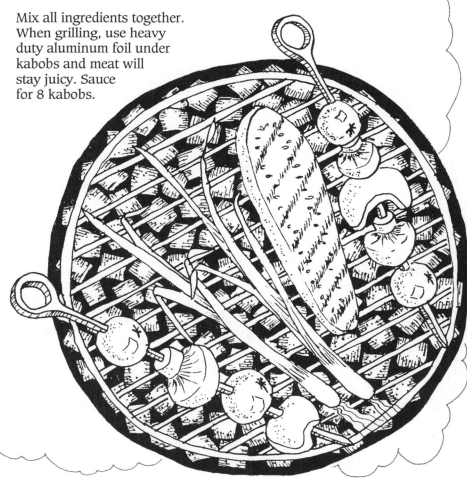

How to "De-Calorize" Your Favorite Dips

Mary K. Murray
Mount Vernon, OH

Everyone has a favorite dip, and what usually makes them so fat-tening is the base. Most dips start out with a sour cream base that's close to 500 calories a cupful or cream cheese at 850 calories per 8 oz. package. If you put mayonnaise in, it's 1600 calories a cupful! The challenge is to duplicate these special flavors with slimmer stand-ins. Here's how:

Mock Sour Cream

For a sour cream-flavored dip base, use "Mock Sour Cream." It's a magic stand-in you can mix up in your blender. Just add 1/4 cup of buttermilk to 1 cup of low-fat cottage cheese. Blend on high, scraping down the container sides often, until the mixture is smooth and creamy. It's so close in taste and texture you can use it on fresh fruits, baked potatoes, or in any recipe that doesn't call for baking. (This "sour cream" can't take the heat!) This recipe makes 1 cup of Mock Sour Cream. You can use in any of the dip recipes on the next page.

Nasturtium Cream Cheese Dip

1/4 lb. low-fat cream cheese
2 t. nasturtium leaves, finely chopped
flowers for decorating

Blend cream cheese and chopped leaves gently. Put into a pretty bowl and decorate with flowers. Serve chilled with favorite toasts or crackers.
Beautiful!

California Dip

1 envelope onion soup dip mix
1 T. dry onion flakes
1 c. mock sour cream (see recipe previous page)

Yields 1 cup. (12 calories per tablespoon)

Cheddar Dip

1/4 c. extra-sharp cheddar   1 T. parsley flakes
    cheese, shredded   1 c. mock sour cream
1/2 t. salt

Yields 1 1/4 cups. (20 calories per serving)

Deviled Ham Dip

2 1/4 oz. can deviled ham   1 c. mock sour cream
1 t. prepared horseradish

Yields 1 1/4 cups. (18 calories per tablespoon)

Crunchy Bacon Dip

1 t. vinegar
1 c. mock sour cream

Just before serving, stir in:

2 T. bacon chips
1 t. garlic salt

Yields 1 cup. (15 calories
per tablespoon)

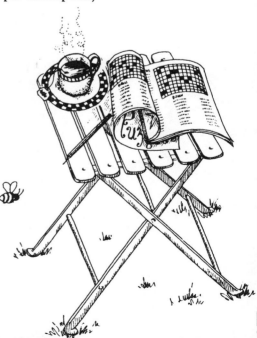

*It's important to keep
your mind active...
work crossword puzzles
and word games.*

Make magic with garnishes

Garnishes are great, because they add fun to your food and make any plate look even more appetizing. It's easy to add some simple elegance to your meal with a few little touches. Here are some ways to make magic with garnishes:

Colorful Citrus Wheels

Slice an orange, a lemon and a lime into 1/4-inch rounds. Cut halfway through each round, to the center. Using two hands, hold each side of the cut slice and twist them in opposite directions so the ends serve as a base, and the top half of the round will stand upright. Place on salad plates, or decorate the rim of a salmon platter. Have fun arranging the colors!

Radish Roses

Clean radishes thoroughly. Trim the top and bottom off the radish so that it's flat on both ends. Cut an X into the top of the radish, making a slice about 3/4 of the way down. Turn the radish and make another X so that you have 8 equal cut portions. Soak covered with ice water for about 20 minutes, and the "roses" will open.

Scallion Starbursts

Trim off bulb and top of scallion. Using a sharp paring knife, make several 1 or 2 inch-long cuts on each end of the scallion, leaving about 2 inches in the middle. Soak for 15 minutes in ice water. The strands will curl open.

Sweet Nothings

Crunchy Chocolate Pie

Pat Akers
Stanton, CA

If you are like me, you can't resist chocolate. This recipe helps me with that craving and also makes a nice dessert without the guilt.

3 T. reduced-fat peanut butter
2 T. honey
2 c. toasted rice cereal
2 c. skim milk

1.5 oz. pkg. reduced-calorie instant chocolate pudding mix

Coat an 8" pie plate with non-stick spray. In a saucepan, warm the peanut butter and honey over low heat until the peanut butter has melted. Remove the pan from the heat. Stir in the cereal. Press the cereal mixture into the bottom and up the sides of the pie plate. Freeze for 1 hour. Using the skim milk, prepare the instant pudding according to the package directions. Immediately pour the pudding into the prepared pie crust. Refrigerate for at least 1 hour before serving. Serves 8.

Matt's Best-Ever
Peanut Butter Pie

Debbie and Matt Ocker
Harrisburg, PA

This pie is a specialty of our nine-year old son. It is an often-requested recipe.

8 oz. pkg. non-fat cream cheese
   or light Neufchatel cheese
1 1/2 c. sugar
1 c. reduced-fat peanut butter
1 c. skim or non-fat milk

16 oz. container light
   whipped topping
2- 9" ready-made
   graham pie crusts
2 T. dry roasted peanuts,
   chopped (optional)

Whip cream cheese and sugar together in large bowl until soft and fluffy. Gradually add peanut butter and milk and beat together at low speed of mixer. Fold in whipped topping. Pour into 2 pie crust shells. Sprinkle tops of pies with chopped peanuts. Put pies in freezer for 3 to 4 hours or overnight. Cut pies while frozen. Makes 2-9" pies. Variation for Chocolate Peanut Butter pie: Use 2-9" chocolate ready-made crusts. Mix same ingredients as above, but pour mixture into chocolate pie shells. Grate a small amount of chocolate on top of the pies, in place of the chopped peanuts.

Apple Pie for One

Jeanne Calkins
Midland, MI

This is tasty recipe for a quick dessert or an evening snack which you've saved calories for.

2 t. reduced-calorie margarine
1 small apple, peeled
   and thinly sliced
1 1/2 t. brown sugar

1/4 t. apple pie spice
1 oz. pita bread

Heat margarine in a small skillet. Brown apple with brown sugar and spices. Stuff into the pita bread. Bake at 350 degrees for 10 minutes or you may microwave for one minute on high. Yields 1 serving.

Sweet Nothings

Easy Pumpkin Pie

Rebecca Suiter
Checotah, OK

Your friends will love this creamy pumpkin pie that doesn't need a crust!

16 oz. can pumpkin
12 oz. can evaporated skim milk
3 egg whites, or 1/2 c. cholesterol-free egg product
1/2 c. sugar
1/2 c. all-purpose flour

1 1/2 t. pumpkin pie spice
3/4 t. baking powder
1/8 t. salt
2 t. orange peel, grated

Brown Sugar Topping:

1/4 c. brown sugar, packed
1/4 c. quick-cooking oats

1 T. margarine, softened

Heat oven to 350 degrees. Spray a 10" pie plate with non-stick cooking spray. Place, in order, pumpkin, skim milk, egg whites or egg product, sugar, flour, pumpkin pie spice, baking powder, salt and grated orange peel in blender or food processor. Cover and blend until smooth. Pour into pie plate. Prepare brown sugar topping by mixing all three ingredients in a small mixing bowl. Sprinkle pie with topping. Bake for 50 to 55 minutes or until knife inserted in center comes out clean. Let cool for 15 minutes. Refrigerate about 4 hours or until chilled. Serves 8. (175 calories with 2 grams of fat per serving)

Skinny Pie Crust

Mary K. Murray
Mount Vernon, OH

1/4 c. diet margarine
1/2 c. all-purpose flour, sifted

1/4 t. salt
1/4 t. baking powder

Soften margarine to room temperature. Sift flour, salt and baking powder together in a deep bowl. Add margarine all at once. Cut with a fork or pastry blender and continue mixing until no pastry sticks to the sides of the bowl. Shape into a ball. Wrap in wax paper and refrigerate until thoroughly chilled, at least 1 hour or more. Makes one crust.

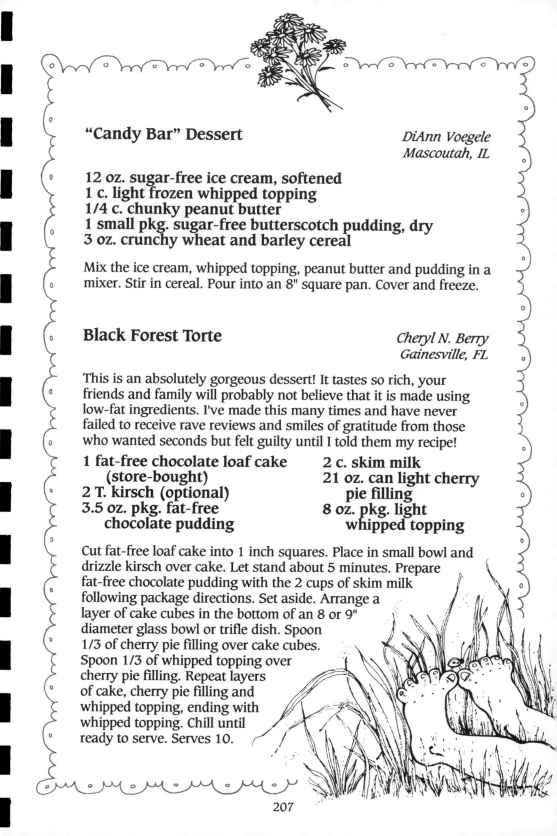

"Candy Bar" Dessert

DiAnn Voegele
Mascoutah, IL

12 oz. sugar-free ice cream, softened
1 c. light frozen whipped topping
1/4 c. chunky peanut butter
1 small pkg. sugar-free butterscotch pudding, dry
3 oz. crunchy wheat and barley cereal

Mix the ice cream, whipped topping, peanut butter and pudding in a mixer. Stir in cereal. Pour into an 8" square pan. Cover and freeze.

Black Forest Torte

Cheryl N. Berry
Gainesville, FL

This is an absolutely gorgeous dessert! It tastes so rich, your friends and family will probably not believe that it is made using low-fat ingredients. I've made this many times and have never failed to receive rave reviews and smiles of gratitude from those who wanted seconds but felt guilty until I told them my recipe!

1 fat-free chocolate loaf cake
   (store-bought)
2 T. kirsch (optional)
3.5 oz. pkg. fat-free
   chocolate pudding

2 c. skim milk
21 oz. can light cherry
   pie filling
8 oz. pkg. light
   whipped topping

Cut fat-free loaf cake into 1 inch squares. Place in small bowl and drizzle kirsch over cake. Let stand about 5 minutes. Prepare fat-free chocolate pudding with the 2 cups of skim milk following package directions. Set aside. Arrange a layer of cake cubes in the bottom of an 8 or 9" diameter glass bowl or trifle dish. Spoon 1/3 of cherry pie filling over cake cubes. Spoon 1/3 of whipped topping over cherry pie filling. Repeat layers of cake, cherry pie filling and whipped topping, ending with whipped topping. Chill until ready to serve. Serves 10.

Sweet Nothings

Low-Fat Chocolate Chip Oatmeal Cookies

Mary Shrank
Santa Clara, CA

4 T. butter or margarine
3/4 c. packed brown sugar
3/4 c. granulated sugar
1/2 c. unsweetened applesauce
2 large egg whites
2 T. water
2 t. vanilla

1 1/4 c. all-purpose flour
3/4 t. baking powder
3/4 t. baking soda
1/2 t. cinnamon
1/4 t. salt
2 1/2 c. rolled oats
1 c. chocolate chips*

Preheat oven to 350 degrees. Spray a baking sheet with non-stick cooking spray. In a large bowl cream butter, brown sugar and granulated sugar until evenly blended. Add applesauce, egg whites, water and vanilla; beat until well mixed. Sift flour with baking powder, baking soda, cinnamon and salt. Add to creamed mixture; beat just until blended. Add rolled oats and beat until oats are well blended. Stir in chocolate chips. Using 1 tablespoon of dough for each cookie, drop 1 1/2" apart on prepared baking sheet. Bake 12 minutes or until cookies are golden brown. Transfer cookies to a rack and let cool. Store in airtight container. Makes 4 dozen 2 1/2" cookies.

*For a healthier cookie, substitute 1 cup of raisins for the chocolate chips.

Guilt-Free Brownies

Mary Bellizzi
Farmingville, NY

1 1/2 c. sugar
1 c. flour
1/3 c. cocoa
1/2 t. baking powder
1/4 t. salt
1/4 c. frozen egg substitute, thawed

1/4 c. water
1 egg white
2 T. margarine
1 T. vanilla extract

Preheat oven to 350 degrees. Combine sugar, flour, cocoa, baking powder and salt. Add egg substitute, water, egg white, margarine and vanilla; stir until well blended. Spoon batter into 8" square baking pan that has been sprayed with non-stick vegetable cooking spray. Bake for 25 to 30 minutes.

Low-Fat Chocolate Chip Cookies

Dawn Weaver
Souderton, PA

Delicious!

1 c. prune puree*
3/4 c. granulated sugar
3/4 c. brown sugar, packed
3 large egg whites
1 t. vanilla

2 1/4 c. flour
1 t. baking soda
1 t. salt
2 c. (12 oz.) semisweet
   chocolate morsels

Preheat oven to 375 degrees. Spray cookie sheet with non-stick spray. In large bowl, beat prune puree, sugars, egg whites and vanilla to blend thoroughly. In a small bowl mix flour, baking soda and salt. Stir dry ingredients into prune mixture, mix completely. Stir in chocolate morsels. Drop by tablespoonfuls onto cookie sheets. Bake 10 minutes.

*prune puree: 4 oz. pitted prunes and 3 T. water, pureed in food processor.

Chocolate-Dipped Strawberries

Debbie Ocker
Harrisburg, PA

This recipe is very easy and gets rave reviews at picnics and parties!

2- 8 oz. containers plain non-fat yogurt
1.4 oz. pkg. chocolate or chocolate fudge fat-free,
   sugar-free instant pudding
1 to 2 qts. fresh strawberries

Put yogurt and dry pudding mix into medium-size bowl. Stir together until pudding mix is combined with yogurt. Chill 1 to 2 hours or over-night. Dip fresh strawberries into dip and enjoy!

Summertime Strawberry Dessert
Donna Scheuerman
Warwick, NY

Once they taste this summertime treat, you will have to make it again and again, but do yourself a favor and double the recipe... there still won't be any leftovers! This summertime salad winds up at every shower, birthday and holiday celebration.

1 large box strawberry gelatin or 2- 3.4 oz. boxes, sugar-free gelatin
1 c. boiling water
1 large pkg. frozen strawberries, thawed
1/2 c. walnuts, chopped
1 small can (5 or 6 oz.) crushed pineapple, drained
2 mashed bananas
1/2 pt. light sour cream

Add boiling water to gelatin; stir until completely dissolved. Add the strawberries to the hot gelatin. Continue by adding the walnuts, pineapple and bananas. Let cool. When partially jelled, pour half into 9"x9" pan. Spread the sour cream and repeat by putting the other half of the gelatin mixture on the top. Refrigerate and cover. Should be made 24 hours before serving. Serves 4 to 6.

Heavenly Strawberry Trifle
Lisa DelPrete
Rockland, MA

1 angel food cake (10 oz.)
1/2 pkg. whipped topping mix (1 envelope)
1/2 c. skim milk
1/2 t. vanilla
1 1/2 c. fat-free vanilla yogurt
1 pt. strawberries, sliced
3 kiwi fruit, sliced
1/4 c. almonds, slivered

Tear cake into 3/4" pieces. Prepare topping mix as directed on package using 1/2 cup skim milk and 1/2 tsp. vanilla. Layer half each of the cake pieces, yogurt, whipped topping, strawberries and kiwi fruit in 2 qt. serving bowl, repeat. Sprinkle with almonds. Refrigerate at least 2 hours. Makes 8 servings.

Blueberry Cake

Beverly Gantar

3 c. flour, sifted, plus sprinkle of
   flour, tossed with blueberries
3 t. baking powder
1 t. salt
2 c. sugar
1 c. milk
2 eggs

1/3 c. oil
1/2 t. vanilla
2 c. blueberries
   (fresh or frozen,
   need not be
   thawed)

Topping:

1/2 c. sugar   3/4 t. nutmeg

Mix dry ingredients in large bowl. Make a well in the center and add liquid ingredients. Mix well (batter is slightly thick). Stir in berries last. Pour into greased and floured 13"x9" pan. Sprinkle topping on unbaked cake. Bake at 350 degrees for 50 minutes.

Low-Fat Chocolate Raspberry Cheesecake

Mary Shrank
Santa Clara, CA

24 plain chocolate
    wafer cookies
2- 8 oz. pkgs. fat-free
    cream cheese
1 c. sugar
1 c. cocoa
1/4 t. salt
1 t. pure vanilla

3 T. sugar-free black
    raspberry preserves
1/2 c. fat-free egg
    substitute
16 oz. container fat-free
    sour cream
non-fat cooking spray

In a food processor or blender, grind the plain chocolate wafers into fine crumbs. Generously coat a 8 1/2" or 9" springform pan with non-stick cooking spray. Pour the crumbs into the pan and tilt to coat bottom and sides evenly. Set aside. Preheat oven to 350 degrees. With an electric mixer, beat the fat-free cream cheese until soft. Add the sugar, cocoa, salt, vanilla and raspberry preserves. Continue beating until the ingredients are incorporated. Add the egg substitute, sour cream and salt, beating until no lumps remain and mixture is smooth and liquid. You may have to beat the mixture for several minutes to reach this consistency. Pour the batter into the prepared pan. Place in oven and immediately reduce oven temperature to 300 degrees. Bake for one hour, or until center is set and firm to the touch. Turn off oven and allow cheesecake to stay in cooling oven for one hour longer. Remove and cool completely. Refrigerate overnight before serving. Serves 10.

Easy Fresh Raspberry Sauce

Kathy Epperly
Wichita, KS

Delicious served over angel food cake or fat-free vanilla yogurt!

2 c. raspberries
1 T. sugar

1 T. lime juice

Combine raspberries, sugar and lime juice in a medium bowl. Mash the berries slightly with a fork and let stand covered at room temperature for one hour. Serves 4.

Lemon Torte with Raspberries

Delores Berg
Selah, WA

4-serving size pkg. low-calorie, lemon-flavored gelatin
1/2 c. boiling water
1/2 of 6 oz. can (1/3 c.) frozen lemonade concentrate, thawed
1 T. sugar
12 oz. can evaporated skim milk
2 c. angel food cake, cubed
2 c. fresh raspberries

Spray bottom of 8" springform pan with non-stick cooking spray. In a large bowl, dissolve lemon gelatin in boiling water. Stir in lemonade, sugar and evaporated milk. Cover and chill in refrigerator for 1 to 1 1/2 hours. After chilling, beat gelatin mixture with electric mixer, on high, for 5 to 6 minutes or until fluffy. Arrange cake cubes in bottom of springform pan. Pour gelatin mixture over cake. Chill for 4 hours. To serve, cut into wedges and spoon raspberries over top. Serves 12. (80 calories per serving)

Raspberry Ice

Deb Weiser
Gooseberry Patch Warehouse

15 oz. can red raspberries or peach slices
2-8 oz. cartons vanilla low-fat yogurt
1 T. honey

Blend raspberries and their juice in blender until smooth. Strain to remove seeds. In bowl mix fruit, yogurt and honey. Pour in 8"x8" pan and freeze. Break up mixture and mix with electric mixer in bowl. Cover and re-freeze for 6 hours. Serve scoops in dessert dishes. Serves 8.

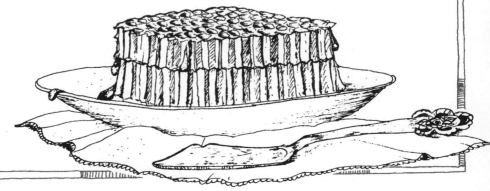

Sweet Nothings

Creamsicle Salad

Sue Carbaugh
Mt. Vernon, WA

Our local deli serves a similar salad that I just love. I came home and tried to re-create it and this is my version. Delicious and low-fat!

1 small box sugar-free orange gelatin (dry mix)
1 small box sugar-free vanilla pudding (dry mix)
1 small can mandarin oranges, drained (reserve liquid)
2 c. miniature marshmallows
12 oz. light whipped topping

In large bowl, mix orange gelatin (dry mix) and vanilla pudding (dry mix). Fold whipped topping into the dry mixes. Add two to four tablespoons reserved mandarin orange liquid; stir well. Add mandarin oranges and miniature marshmallows until well-blended. Chill. Top with extra mandarin orange segments and fresh mint, if desired. Yields 8 to 10 servings.

Yummy Yummy Fruit Dip

Judye Witt
Marlton, NJ

Simple, yummy and healthy! The best part is it is very low-fat and fun for the kids to help make.

1 large container marshmallow fluff
8 oz. pkg. low-fat cream cheese (Neufchatel cheese)
your favorite summer fruits (cut into shapes or pieces)

Combine fluff and cheese; beat with mixer until smooth. Put into bowl. Arrange fruits around it, and there it is! Serve cold on those hot summer nights. Enjoy with melon, canteloupe, oranges, strawberries, pineapple, apples, peaches, nectarines, papaya, grapes, bananas!

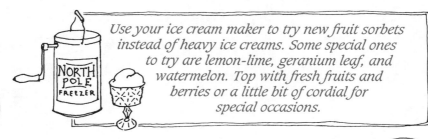

Use your ice cream maker to try new fruit sorbets instead of heavy ice creams. Some special ones to try are lemon-lime, geranium leaf, and watermelon. Top with fresh fruits and berries or a little bit of cordial for special occasions.

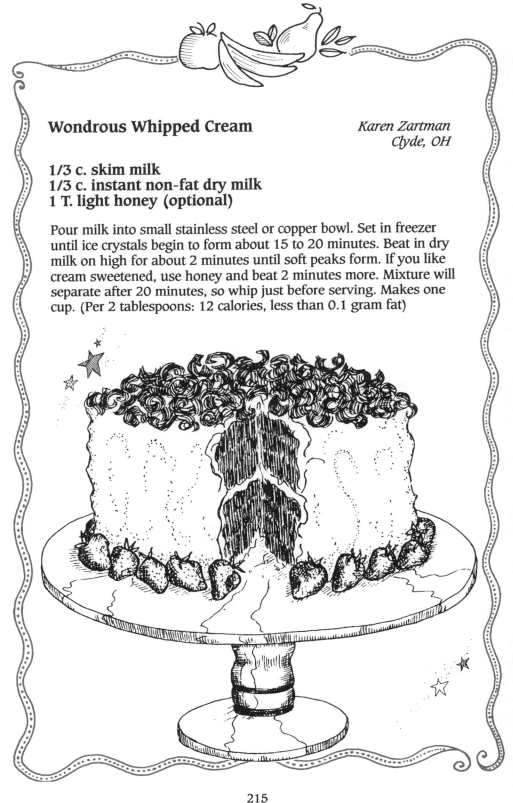

Wondrous Whipped Cream

Karen Zartman
Clyde, OH

1/3 c. skim milk
1/3 c. instant non-fat dry milk
1 T. light honey (optional)

Pour milk into small stainless steel or copper bowl. Set in freezer until ice crystals begin to form about 15 to 20 minutes. Beat in dry milk on high for about 2 minutes until soft peaks form. If you like cream sweetened, use honey and beat 2 minutes more. Mixture will separate after 20 minutes, so whip just before serving. Makes one cup. (Per 2 tablespoons: 12 calories, less than 0.1 gram fat)

Sweet Nothings

Jenni's Frozen Fruit Pops

Liz Roundtree
Petersburg, AK

2 bananas, peeled and halved
2 ripe kiwi fruit, peeled and halved
2/3 c. fresh or frozen strawberries

1/2 c. orange juice
3 T. light corn syrup
6 wooden popsicle sticks

Place bananas, kiwi, strawberries and orange juice in freezer for several hours. Take out and put in blender with corn syrup. Blend until mixed thoroughly. Pour into medium-size paper cups. When partially frozen, put in sticks and freeze until hard. When serving, tear off paper cup and enjoy a healthy, but fun snack! You may try other fruits and berries, but always use bananas for good consistency. Makes 6.

Low-Fat Peach Cobbler

Rebecca Suiter
Checotah, OK

1 1/2 c. low or no-fat biscuit mix
1 1/4 c. evaporated skim milk

1/8 c. sugar

Filling:

4 c. frozen or fresh peaches, sliced
1 t. butter-flavored sprinkles

1 t. lemon juice
3/4 c. sugar

Preheat oven to 350 degrees. Combine filling ingredients. Stir gently until sugar starts to dissolve and set aside. Combine biscuit mix and evaporated skim milk and stir until well blended. Mixture will be like a thin batter. Add sugar and mix. Pour half of the batter into a 13"x9" baking dish that has been sprayed with a non-stick cooking spray. Spoon filling mixture evenly over top. Pour remaining batter over top of filling layer. Sprinkle a spoonful of granulated sugar over top. Bake at 350 degrees for 30 minutes. Serve hot or cold. Serves 8 to 12.

Orange-Pineapple Poppy Seed Bread

Yvonne Van Brimmer
Lompoc, CA

2 c. whole wheat pastry flour
1 T. poppy seeds
1/2 c. sugar

1 t. baking soda
1 c. orange-pineapple juice
1 t. vanilla extract

Combine all dry ingredients and stir to mix well. Add liquids and stir just until moistened. Spray an 8"x4" loaf pan with non-stick cooking spray. Spread mixture evenly in pan. Bake at 325 degrees for 45 minutes. Test center with cake tester or wooden toothpick. It should be clean after being inserted in center of bread. Let sit for 10 minutes, remove from pan and cool on wire rack before slicing. To save more calories, serve with fat-free cream cheese. Yields 1 loaf.

Take a day to window shop.
Getting out in the fresh air, browsing and
people-watching will lift your spirits. You'll get
lots of ideas for decorating your home and
freshening up your wardrobe.

CORN

TOMATO

PEAS

INDEX

INDEX

Gooseberry Patch Originals

Reserve your copies today!

Homespun Christmas

Treasured family recipes, memories, homemade decorations, heartfelt gifts & holiday traditions

HOMESPUN CHRISTMAS A heartwarming collection of Christmas recipes, tips and ideas

Celebrate Spring

A freshly gathered bouquet of tender recipes, brand new how-tos and tempting tips for the joyous days of springtime

Collect the WHOLE Set!

Celebrate Summer

A star-spangled collection of luscious recipes, carefree tips and easy how-tos for long, lazy summer days.

Celebrate Autumn

A bushel of fresh-picked fall recipes, tips & how-to's for the festive season of friends & family

Celebrate Winter

A warmhearted collection of recipes for joyful holidays, sparkling celebrations & cozy fireside feasts

Gooseberry Patch Originals

WELCOME HOME for the HOLIDAYS

your companion from September through December

Welcome Home For The Holidays

from harvest through Christmas, tips, a treasury of holiday recipes, decorating traditions & easy-to-make gifts

Old-Fashioned, Country Christmas

A holiday keepsake of recipes, traditions, homemade gifts, decorating ideas, a favorite childhood memories

OLD-FASHIONED COUNTRY COOKIES hundreds of recipes, tips, & ideas

Old-Fashioned Country Cookies

Yummy recipes, tips, traditions, how-to's and sweet memories... everything Cookies

OLD-FASHIONED COUNTRY CHRISTMAS our all-time BEST SELLER!

GOOD FOR YOU! recipes, fun ideas, heartwarming stories, good for body, mind, soul

For Bees & Me

FOR BEES & ME garden-fresh recipes, backyard entertaining & gifts from the garden

A Bouquet of garden-fresh recipes, berries, herbs, Simple Pleasures, Herbal Beauty Patterns, backyard Entertainment & Easy-to-Make Gifts

Good For You!

A collection of good food, good fun, good stories for the body, mind & soul!

friends ▣ energetic exercise family fun ✿ crafts

star gazing ☆ bedtime stories warm offerings bike rides shared recipes

old moonlight walks ❋ childhood dreams fresh veggies creative cooking

tasty dishes favorite songs giggles more

A Country Store In Your Mailbox®

Gooseberry Patch
149 Johnson Drive
Department BOOK
Delaware, OH 43015

Please send me the following Gooseberry Patch books:

Book	Quantity	Price	Total
Old-Fashioned Country Christmas	_____	$14.95	_____
Welcome Home for the Holidays	_____	$14.95	_____
Old-Fashioned Country Cookies	_____	$14.95	_____
For Bees & Me	_____	$17.95	_____
Good For You!	_____	$14.95	_____
Homespun Christmas	_____	$14.95	_____
Celebrate Spring	_____	$12.95	_____
Celebrate Summer	_____	$12.95	_____
Celebrate Autumn	_____	$12.95	_____
Celebrate Winter	_____	$12.95	_____
Coming Home for Christmas	_____	$14.95	_____
Family Favorites	_____	$14.95	_____

Merchandise Total _____

Ohio Residents add 6 1/4% _____

Shipping & handling: Add $2.50 for each book. Call for special delivery prices.

Total _____

Quantity discounts and special shipping prices available when purchasing 6 or more books. Call and ask! Wholesale inquiries invited.

Name: _____

Address: _____

City: _____ State: _____ Zip: _____

We accept checks, money orders, Visa or MasterCard (please include expiration date).
Payable in U.S. funds only. Prices subject to change.

friends energetic exercise family fun crafts

star gazing bedtime stories warm offerings bike rides shared recipes

tasty dishes favorite songs giggles & more

creative cooking fresh veggies childhood dreams moonlight walks old